CAPTURING THE YOUNGER BROTHERS GANG IN THE NORTHERN PLAINS

CAPTURING THE YOUNGER BROTHERS GANG IN THE NORTHERN PLAINS

THE UNTOLD STORY OF HEROIC TEEN ASLE SORBEL

ARLEY KENNETH FADNESS

THE History PRESS

Published by The History Press
Charleston, SC
www.historypress.com

First published 2022

Manufactured in the United States

ISBN 9781467152365

Library of Congress Control Number: 2022933327

To my new granddaughter, baby girl Ela Rae, daughter of Joel and Beth.

CONTENTS

ACKNOWLEDGEMENTS

My profound and deserving thanks I give to many former and new supportive friends in writing this book. I am thankful to the descendants of Asle Oscar Sorbel who have supplied me with newly unearthed primary sources. Thanks to granddaughters Mary Lou Harpstead and Dorothy Nilsen, and the late Evelyn Sorbel Boyer; grandsons Herbert Sorbel, David Sorbel, Robert Sorbel and the late Jan Sorbel; and great-grandson Stanley Harpstead.

I have graciously received stories, photographs and various informative documents and artifacts from Bradley and Kristine Hovland from Rapid City, South Dakota; Paul and Karen Larson from Custer, South Dakota; and Asle Sorbel's grandson Dan Sorbel from Rapid City. Dan shared with me his insights on numerous interviews and displayed the ring his grandfather purchased with the reward money he (Asle) had received for helping capture the Younger brothers' outlaw gang.

Surprised, intrigued and compelled, I engaged in a historic and literary quest because one character (Asle Oscar Sorbel) in Mark Gardner's book *Shot All to Hell*, was, in fact, a hero from my hometown of Webster, South Dakota. I never knew it. Most Webster citizens didn't know it. But now I do. And they will know it by this publication. And so will you my devoted readers. I appreciate and thank many generous donors in this literary quest. Sister Oriette Fadness Rentschler provided a photo of our father, Lawrence Fadness, who was a horseman, leading us to speculate Lawrence had been a client of Doc Sorbel. Thanks to Susan Hvistendahl of Northfield; to Myrna Wey of Green Mountain, Colorado, whose father, Oscar Lindholm, knew Doc Sorbel and kept notes about him. Thanks to Amanda Fanger of the *Reporter and Farmer*, who helped facilitate my "Webster Bandit Buster" presentation a few years back and provided me with contemporary photos. Mange Takk to Duane Anderson, curator of the Webster Wildlife and Industry Museum. I enjoyed and learned important points through personal conversations with nonfiction writer Wayne Fanebust, author of *Chasing Frank and Jesse James*. I am profoundly grateful to the late John Klobas and North Star Press for valuable resources and stories, particularly in *The Great Cole Younger & Frank James Historical Wild West Show*, *Minnesota Grit* and *When the Heavens Fell: The Youngers in Stillwater Prison*.

I am grateful for the assistance from Pam Sandbo and Barb Nelson at the Watonwan County Historical Museum in Madelia, Minnesota; support from Doris Ann Mertz, Jan Stadler, and Mary Richards at the Custer County Library; Gary Enright, former director of the Custer County Courthouse Museum in Custer, South Dakota; and Jeanne Kirkpatrick, present director.

For the cordial help with securing interlibrary resources from the Siouxland Library Ronning Branch staff, namely Jane, Joe, Alisha, Courtney and Jeri and others, I am profoundly indebted.

I was so happy to receive research assistance from Kari Mahowald, Liz Cisar and Dr. Harry Thompson at the Center for Western Studies at Augustana University, Sioux Falls, South Dakota. Thanks to the staff at the Mikkelson Library at Augustana University for borrowed resources.

I am grateful for the South Dakota Humanities Council. The council provides a platform for my presentations as a humanities scholar, engaging history buffs in communities throughout South Dakota, Iowa and Minnesota.

Thanks to Stephan Barrett and Cathy Osterman, collections managers at the Northfield Historical Society, for photos. Thanks for photos from Bradley Boner for the Jesse James Inn stay.

Thanks to Katie Worth from Fairmont, Minnesota, for the book *Early History of Lincoln County, Minnesota*, by Tasker.

And to my friend Sam Hatlestad, I give a mile-wide smile for his offer to read, critique and advise me in my early drafts. My thanks also to lifelong friends Charles Berdahl, Lyle Rossing, and Chuck Christensen for their perusal of early manuscripts.

Other support I applaud came from the Library of Congress, Jackson County Historical Society in Missouri, Missouri Historical Society, Brown County Historical Society, Washington County Historical Society, South Dakota Historical Society, theMinnesota Historical Society and Rice County Historical Society

INTRODUCTION
A SECRET UNFOLDS

Secrets, silent, stony sit in the dark places of both our hearts:
secrets weary of their tyranny:
Tyrants willing to be dethroned.
—James Joyce, Ulysses

Three may keep a secret, if two of them are dead.
—Ben Franklin's Poor Richard's Almanac

Welcome to an untold story that begins in peaceful Norway, travels to two places in Minnesota—where .44 Smith & Wessons blast the silence—and then ends up being told by no one and nearly lost in a cloud of secrecy in South Dakota.

Fragments of this story have been tossed to the wind by hundreds of writers in a maze of literary treasures, both dime novels as well as informative, scholarly and historically researched books by recent authors such as John Koblas, Mark Gardner and Wayne Fanebust. Eternal, it seems, is the fascination and mystique surrounding Jesse and Frank James and the Younger brothers. Myth, legend and history merge as various versions of the truth drift in and out like feathery clouds.

Finally comes the rest of the story about one figure, Norwegian Asle Oscar Sorbel, who played a significant role in the demise of this infamous outlaw gang.

As a metal detector sniffs treasures, I discovered a treasure-trove digging into unpublished memoirs from several descendants of Asle Oscar Sorbel.

We follow this amazing storyline, beginning with the Scandinavian diaspora sailing the Atlantic in the Great Norwegian Migration. We revisit the Northfield botched raid of 1876 by the Jesse James/Younger brothers' outlaw gang. We follow the escape and chase through the Big Woods of Minnesota. We watch the "Paul Revere ride" of Asle Sorbel to Madelia, followed by the shootout and capture of the Younger brothers and their eventual imprisonment. We puzzle at the disappearance of Asle and are surprised at his reappearance as Dr. A.O. Sorbel in an unlikely place. Our story gains momentum filled with new oddities as it follows the dual narratives of Doc Sorbel and Cole Younger from 1883 to 1930.

The Great Migration of Norwegians to America in the nineteenth century began as one of the greatest movements of peoples in modern history. The migration was small at first—only a dribbling stream in 1825. Fifty-two Norwegians struck out into the unknown in a sloop called *The Restoration* on July 4. The sloop was only twenty-six feet by ninety feet. It left from Stavanger, Norway. Historians would proudly give it a moniker, the "Norwegian *Mayflower*." This trickling migration stream would swell into more than one million Norwegian immigrants who would follow, fired by the gallantry and venturesome spirit of the early Vikings. Sailing into the unknown, they would come from Trondheim, Voss, Lillehammer, Oslo, Hallingdal and Sigdahl and a thousand farmsteads and fishing villages throughout the mountains, coastlands and fjord-sprinkled regions.

Moving to America in the nineteenth century, however, was not unique to the Norwegians. Immigration to the new land expanded into a mighty flood of Irish, Germans, Poles, Swedes, Danes, Greeks, Italians, Hungarians, Lebanese, Syrians and scores of others.

This story is about one of those Norwegian families, Ole Sorbel and Guri Redholen, who emigrated from Hallingdal and Sigdahl, Norway. It is about their journey, their landing in America, homesteading and farming Minnesota prairies.

But then the narrative pivots into a dramatic turn of events, interrupting their lives and dreams. Their son Asle Oscar Sorbel was thrust into a swirling dervish as a key player in the capture of the Younger brothers of the Jesse

James/Younger brothers outlaw gang. It happened near sleepy Hanska Slough on September 21, 1876.

But now, lest one simply suspect a regurgitation of oft-told events, our focus takes us beyond the shooting and blasting at the botched Northfield bank raid. It ushers us through the events of the infamous Madelia shootout and equally dramatic capture of the Younger brothers involving Asle Sorbel and the Madelia "Magnificent Seven." Our journey in this piece replays those earlier Wild West historic events briefly, and intentionally, solely for the purpose of context.

The rest of the story is here. It has waited far too long to be discovered and told.

Because of new primary sources and years of detective work, we unearth and celebrate the courage and daring nerve of this plucky, fearless seventeen-year-old Norwegian lad—the key player in the capture.

This story is about secrets: many devious secrets and deceptions by the outlaws, Cole Younger's lifelong secrets and the big secret Asle Oscar Sorbel carried in his soul for the rest of his life.

Lips tight as a sprung bear trap. Arms folded close to the chest. Stubborn resolve.

Young Asle Sorbel (pronounced As-lee Sor-bull) kept the secret all of his life. He had to! For his own safety and for the protection of his family. Friends of the outlaws were planning reprisals. He changed his name, he changed his persona, he changed his location. He kept his mount shut. Vigilant fear haunted him all the rest of his life.

What events would drive a seventeen-year-old second-generation Norwegian lad from rural Madelia, Minnesota, to such desperate and drastic measures?

I tell you, reader, the true tale that follows is about the rest of the story—untold in prior publications. New primary sources uncovered, organized and flung to the public are yours. This tale is about *many* secrets, but especially Sorbel's big secret—only officially revealed to the public in 1924 and then at the end of Asle Oscar Sorbel's life in 1929.

Other, less honorable secrets were kept close inside their ulster duster garments. Eight outlaws left Missouri on their way to do outlawry and mayhem in Minnesota. The Civil War had ended more than a decade before the James Younger Gang rode north. But the war was not really over in their minds. Bitterness and resentment called for retribution. Vengeance and avarice would be meted out by revolver—and violence.

Jesse and Frank James; Cole, Bob and Jim Younger; Clell Miller; Charlie Pitts; and Bill Chadwell—no gang of criminals more feared, more hunted,

Modern photo of Lemon farm where Cole Younger and gang stopped near Lake Benton on their way to do a little banking in Northfield. *Courtesy of* The Early History of Lincoln County, Minnesota *by A.E. Tasker and provided by later farm family member Katie Worth.*

more hated, more admired and more celebrated—were about to do their "thing." Above all, they had secret plans they must make happen, or else.

One day in August 1876, strangers arrived at a farmstead near Lake Benton, Minnesota. It was the home of Hans Gran, homesteaded by Thomas Lemon and later known as the Nordmeyer farmstead.

When I visited the Lemon farm on many occasions, it was owned and operated by my parishioners and friends Clarence and Evelyn Worth and their two children, Leonard and Barbara.

Precisely one hundred years before my visits with the Worths, ghostly strangers came dressed in long linen dusters on fine horses. Dusters were perfect, loose-fitting garments for cowboys offering protection from dust and grime while also hiding large single-action army .44 Colts and Smith & Wesson model #3 revolvers. These large, ivory-gripped, cleaned and oiled armaments, ready to be cocked and fired, lay asleep in leather holsters. Also, ample cowhide ammunition belts to replenish spent bullets were concealed from sight.

In the *Early History of Lincoln County*, A.E. Tasker recounts,

> *It is a well known historical fact that members of the notorious James and Younger gangsters entered Minnesota sometime in the month of August, 1876, in different groups and from different points. According to information related to us by the Kelley brothers, a group of this robber gang, supposedly headed by Cole Younger, passed through Lake Benton sometime during the month of August, 1876, and passed on to the east some three weeks or thereabouts, previous to the Northfield bank robbery.…The group of men halted their horses and one of the group acted as spokesman and who, the brothers (Kelley) afterwards decided, must have been Cole Younger from his appearance coinciding with published descriptions of him. He was very courteous and kindly spoken.…The above group of men rode on to the home of Hans Gran…and there received food and evidently proceeded to the Lemon home on the south side of the lake about four miles northeast to Lake Benton, where they again procured refreshments.*[1]

The Lake Benton sightings were among many actual—and just as many conjectured—glimpses that happened after the James and Younger brothers' northern journey had begun in early August 1876.

All eight desperadoes boarded a passenger train from St. Joseph, Missouri, rolling north to Sioux City, Iowa, about 226 miles. The journey hugged the Missouri River Valley. From Sioux City, they boarded the St. Paul and Sioux City Railroad. After another 280 miles, they landed in Minneapolis/St Paul.

It was Wednesday, August 23, 1876, when they checked into the Nicollet House in Minneapolis. The next day, other gang members appeared and also wrote false names in the same register. The eight travelers, striking and distinct, wearing their boots, wide-brimmed hats and confident swagger, caught the eyes of many Twin City folks.

On Thursday, August 24, Jesse, Frank, Clell and Jim spent a weekend in Red Wing, Minnesota. There at J.A. Anderberg's Livery Stable they purchased four horses. They carefully selected a nine-year-old bay mare, a five-year-old gelding and two sorrel horses from A. Seebeck, a well-known horse dealer in the Red Wing area. Next they visited E.P. Watson's Harness Shop. They purchased three new saddles, apparently retaining the fourth from before.[2]

While making these preparations, the gang plotted. They scouted around. They told lies. They practiced the art of deception wherever they went. They investigated and researched, looking for fat and vulnerable banks to rob.

On August 28–29, Bob Younger and Bill Chadwell, still in St. Paul, purchased strong, swift steeds to ride. Cole and Charlie Pitts traveled to St. Peter.

Millersburg Store, which the gang patronized on their way to raid the bank in Northfield. *Courtesy of the Rice County Historical Society.*

The gang spent the last week in August in St. Peter, Minnesota, and while they were exercising and training their horses, a little girl ran up to Cole and said she could ride horseback. Cole stopped, pulling back on the horse's reins; he tenderly reached down and picked up the surprised but pleased little girl. She told Cole her name was Horace Greeley Perry. He complimented her, and when he set her down, she announced, "I won't always be little. I will be a newspaper man like my pa." This incident turned out to be a key coincidence. Little Horace Greeley Perry would one day become the editor of the St. Peter, Minnesota newspaper and a vocal proponent and champion for the Younger brothers when they were seeking parole and pardon from Stillwater Prison.

On September 2, five outlaws arrived in Mankato to make serious plans to rob one of two banks. But they were spooked by the large crowd, which had gathered in front of one bank for otherwise innocent reasons.

They left Mankato quickly and headed east. On September 6, the day before their plans unfolded, Cole, Jim, Clell and Pitts stayed in Millersburg near Northfield, Minnesota. Jesse, Frank, Bob and Bill stayed at Cannon City.

When next morning, tectonic Thursday, September 7, 1876, came, a volcano erupted, spewing hot magma on the streets of Northfield.

The journey of the outlaws from Missouri and the Twin Cities to Mankato, including not only the Lake Benton visit but also several other sightings and stopovers, headed east. The outlaws rode on horses and in trains and trekked through farms, villages and cities throughout south-central Minnesota. They moved about, spouting convenient ruses as land speculators, cattle buyers, hunters and fishermen. Hardly noticed by anyone or viewed with

The Cushman Hotel, where the gang stayed overnight in Millersburg. The Cushman Hotel also served as the Millersburg post office. *Courtesy of the Rice County Historical Society.*

overt suspicions they traveled from Minneapolis, St. Paul, to Cleveland, to St. Peter, Le Sueur, Janesville, Cordova, Cannon City, to Mankato and ultimately to Northfield, busy spying, lying, plotting and practice shooting.

Fast-forward, after the debacle at Northfield, the unintended destination would end near the little town of Madelia—at least for the Younger brothers and Charlie Pitts. Jesse and Frank James, by stealth, luck and grit, had escaped. There it unfolded near Madelia, Minnesota, the details of the untold big secret of Asle Oscar Sorbel.

PROLOGUE
AMERICA BOUND

Many and incredible are the tales the grandfathers tell from those days when the wilderness was yet untamed, and when they unwittingly founded the Kingdom.
—O.E. Rølvaag, Giants in the Earth

The ways of the pioneer is always rough.
—Harvey S. Firestone

To cross the Atlantic Ocean in the 1840s was no walk in the park. It was a rodeo! Bucking and snorting. It was a plunge, a thrust, a harrowing, dangerous ride. The wind stirred up angry waves—waves producing mini mountains and deep gorges. The schooner leaned and listed, bobbed and weaved. White-faced passengers clung to fife rails, lanyard ropes, spar and one another to avoid being thrown to the deck or flung into the sea.

Then the waves would go calm. Mother Nature brought a welcome serenity. The smooth seas and cordial sun offered travelers like Ole Sorbel, twenty-two, and his wife (surmised to be "Julie") and two boys, Stor Ole and Lill Ole, a brief pause to relax and even to dream of the future. But why did emigrants, like Ole Sorbel and his family, long for a new future? Why did they leave a safe, beautiful country in order to settle permanently in another? There was tranquility back in Hallingdal, Norway. The expansive Hallingdal Valley lay in eastern Norway near Skøgshørn Mountain. There in Hallingdal, farmers trekked up the mountains in the summer to green pastures to graze their livestock. The women turned their herds loose and stayed with them for the summer. In the Norwegian language, this time and place was called a seter, a "vacation place." The air was light, and the sun shone more hours in the day there than down between the mountain walls of the valley farms. The grass, so very sweet and nourishing, carpeted the steppes. They made the finest butter and cheese.

So why leave?

The reasons why Ole and Julie's family decided to immigrate to the new world will likely never be known. Great-granddaughter Mary Lou Harpestead, in her recollections titled *From Norway to Home*, gives many details of the Ole Sorbel odyssey but no definitive answer to the "why."

It is well-known and documented why many thousands of Norwegians decided to leave their homeland and sail for America. Civil and religious Norwegian authorities were oppressive. Religious groups like the Quakers and the followers of Hans Nielsen Hauge found the State Evangelical Lutheran Church constraining and rigid. For a vast majority of the Norwegian farming community, poverty was rampant. Many suffered from the potato blight in 1845. In 1866–68, widespread famine struck, causing immeasurable hardships. There was limited land. Confounding progress, standing stubbornly glared the old, restrictive law of primogeniture (ødelsret). This tradition of inheritance rights belonging to the eldest son resulted in only small arable land holdings for large families.

Many left Norway in search for a better life. Others fled because they were hungry for jobs and eager to own land, which sold for $1.25 an acre in America. Who could avoid being smitten by the "American Dream"? Still others were fired with the blood of adventure and freedom in their veins.

Most of all, who could resist the ideal that everyone has an equal chance in America?

From 1836 to 1849, there were 107 Norwegian vessels that made the trip to America. They carried emigrants, iron cargo and supplies needed in the new world.

One ship that sailed ten years earlier than Ole Sorbel's vessel was the bark *Aegir*, which departed Bergen on April 7, 1837, with eighty-four passengers. One passenger on the *Aegir* was Ole Rynning.

After arriving and traveling in America, Rynning wrote a popular and positive handbook titled *True Account of America* (*Sandfaerdig Beretning om Amerika*). This work gave practical information and courage to thousands of Norwegian peasants who were eager to dream about their chances in this new world. Ole Rynning's handbook was not a travelogue but a helpful question-

and-answer style dialogue to deal with the fears of any prospective emigrant. Whether Ole Sorbel had access to this helpful and exciting encouragement we do not know. Nonetheless, when threats and dangers loomed in talk and general conversation, Ole Rynning's writings provided an inspiring antidote.

His practical advice guided the emigrants as they prepared to go to America. He wrote, "They must have provisions to take care of their needs for twelve weeks, particularly foods that could be kept a long time without being spoiled." He suggested "pork, dried meat, salted meat, dried herring, smoked herring, dried fish, butter, cheese, primost, milk, beer, flour, peas, cereals, rye rusks, coffee, tea, sugar," There was danger of sickness on the voyage, so he advised "a little brandy, vinegar, and a couple of bottles of wine, as well as raisins and prunes to make soup for the seasick; a cathartic; sulfur powder and ointment for the itch; Hoffman's drops and spirits of camphor." Ole Rynning went on: the emigrant "must take with him bedclothes, clothing of fur and homespun, an iron plate for baking flat bread, a spinning wheel, a hand mill, silverware and tobacco pipes to sell in America." The men must also take "good rifles, with percussion locks, and tools of his trade." Throughout the winter, "the women of the family spun, wove and sewed dresses, suits, underclothing, and other garments." The men "turned to carpentry, sawing, planing and hammering as they made the many traveling chests required, all with homemade iron bands, locks and large keys."

Ole Sorbel, his family and his fellow emigrants courageously took the leap to leave the motherland. They braved the hazards on what was typically a fifty-three-plus-day journey from Norway to America.

Theodore C. Blegen offers insights on typical voyages in his two-volume book *Norwegian Migration to America: The American Transition*:

> *In prolonged storms, the passengers in steerage* [the cargo area below deck where most were expected to travel]…*could not even get on deck. Down in their quarters pails, cans, pots, kettles, and everything else left unleashed would rattle about and create a perfect pandemonium. All that the poor occupants could do was to cling fast to the nearest post or bed rail and stay there until the rolling ceased somewhat. Oftentimes there was an intense darkness as the hatches had to be closed to exclude the furious sea and save the passengers from drowning. They were unaccustomed to the roll of the ship and there was a vast amount of seasickness, especially among the women. After a storm, when the hatches were opened, people came stumbling out, gasping for air, and the steerage was most frightening and sickening to behold.*

Not only were there dangerous storms at sea, but also sickness on boats took its toll. Blegen notes,

> *It often happened that terrible disease would break out, and spread with appalling speed. Dysentery added to the torment of the emigrants. In one case, it began in the upper bunk aft and continued regularly on starboard until it jumped over larboard and there spread in the same manner. Cholera, typhus, smallpox, typhoid fever and measles were some of the diseases that raged onboard emigrant vessels.*

Ole Sorbel's wife, Julie, grew sick and died. She was buried at sea (according to one source). Her grave would be the unforgiving Atlantic Ocean. Sometimes carpenters would make a wooden casket out of planks, drill holes in it and fill the bottom with sand so that it would sink. One emigrant woman named Olaug Respergaarden died on another vessel. When they buried her at sea, they tied a heavy stone to her ankles. At other times, bodies were wrapped in canvas and weighted down with rocks to make them sink with a spiral motion into the trackless deep.

Ole Sorbel, now a widower, grieving, would continue toward America with his two small sons.

As the ship neared the shores of New York, little did Ole Sorbel dare to even fantasize in his wildest dreams that one of his future sons, Asle Oscar Sorbel, would one day make a profound mark in American history and specifically in the wild, wild West.

One momentous day, Ole Sorbel's seventeen-year-old son would be a part of a historic shootout. Guns would blaze away against the notorious Jesse James/Younger brothers outlaw gang. And because of this historic event and his involvement, Asle would carry a secret the rest of his life. This story is about that secret and how one day it would be revealed.

Ole's family landed on American soil. They, along with hundreds of other Scandinavians, sought a bountiful fortune in a new land.

Widower Ole Sorbel headed west. He traveled to Milwaukee, Wisconsin, and left his two boys there. They were adopted out and moved to North Dakota. For several years, Ole worked with a U.S. government survey team. He plotted lands as far west as the Sioux River near where Sioux Falls, South Dakota, was later established. He filed a land claim in Brown County, Minnesota, in 1854 and settled near Madelia, Minnesota, on farm acreage not far from Linden Lake.

Above: Sketch of an archival photo of Mr. and Mrs. Ole Sorbel about 1875. *Original courtesy of Mary Harpestead's* From Norway to Home, *sketched by author.*

Left: Sorbel family Norwegian Bible. *Courtesy of Asle and Tomina's great-grandson Stanley Harpestead, from the Harpestead Collection.*

Record page of Sorbel Bible. *Courtesy of Stanley Harpestead.*

Ole Sorbel sent for his late wife's sister, Guri Asledatter Redelen, from Sigdal, Norway. After she arrived, they married in the 1850s and proceeded to have eight children—Ole Jr., Asle Oscar, Martin, Gunnil, Siri, Martin, Elisa and Oletta. (The first Martin died, so there is a second Martin.)

The Sorbel family Bible's record page reads,

> *Our first son Ole was born into the world on the 21st of December, 1857. Our second son Asle was born on the 9th of March, 1859. Our third son Martin Edevart was born the 17th of February, 1862 and died on the 16th of September, 1862. Our daughter Gunnil Maria was born the 5th of August, 1863. Our daughter Siri Bergite was born the 12th of March, 1865. Our fourth son, Martin Edevart, was born the 14th of December, 1866. Our daughter Elisa Helena was born the 10th of August 1869. Our fourth daughter was born the 23rd of January, Olette Julia, 1872.* [Courtesy of Norwegian translator Judy Stadem]

Life was good. Life was productive. Ole, Guri and the children cared for the bawling calves, sturdy plow horses, squealing pigs and uncomplaining sheep. There were row gardens to weed and fields of corn, wheat, oats and barley to harvest. There were chores in the morning and evening—milking

Children of Ole and Guri Sorbel, circa 1867. *Left to right*: Ole, Gunnil and Asle. *Courtesy of Mary Harpestead's* From Norway to Home *and Harpestead Collection.*

South Sørbøl farm in Norway where Ole was born. *Photograph taken in 1982, compliments of the late Jan Sorbel in* The Sorbels Then and Now.

contented cows and feeding hungry livestock. Someone must churn the butter, do the canning, make the soap, prepare the cheese, card and spin the wool, dye the fabric and haul the water. All was serene and calm, so it seemed, until one explosive day—September 21, 1876

The name Sorbel is spelled Sørbøl in Norway. Sør means "south." Bøl means "living place." Sørbøl was the name of the farm where Ole was born. Norway is unique in that it is characterized by a "Farm Name" system. According to Oluf Rygh's research published as an encyclopedia of nineteen volumes, *Norske Gaardnavne*, this system established 45,000 farm names, which served as addresses. Some of the main farm names were designated by the government as much as 1,500 years earlier. The Sorbel name is the only place with the Sorbel name, although there was a South and a North Sorbel farm place. Ole came from the South. Ole also used the name Suburn, Ølsgaard and sometimes just plain Ole Oleson. The *gaard* part of Ølsgaard means "farm." Most immigrants dropped the farm name when they came to America. Ole was one of only four or five out of every one hundred immigrants to keep the farm name.

Besides local dialects, Norway has two official languages. They are Nynorsk, the older language spoken in farm areas, and Riksmaal, a Norwegian form of Danish.

Ole and his Guri came to Linden Township in 1857 in a prairie schooner wagon drawn by oxen. This prairie schooner wagon served as a living room and sleeping quarters until a log cabin could be built. Since timber was limited in the Linden area, other settlers lived in dugouts or sod huts until wood could be secured from New Ulm. Ole, fortunately, had black walnut trees on his land to harvest and use to build his cabin. The cabin measured sixteen by twenty feet. (See plan and photo below.)

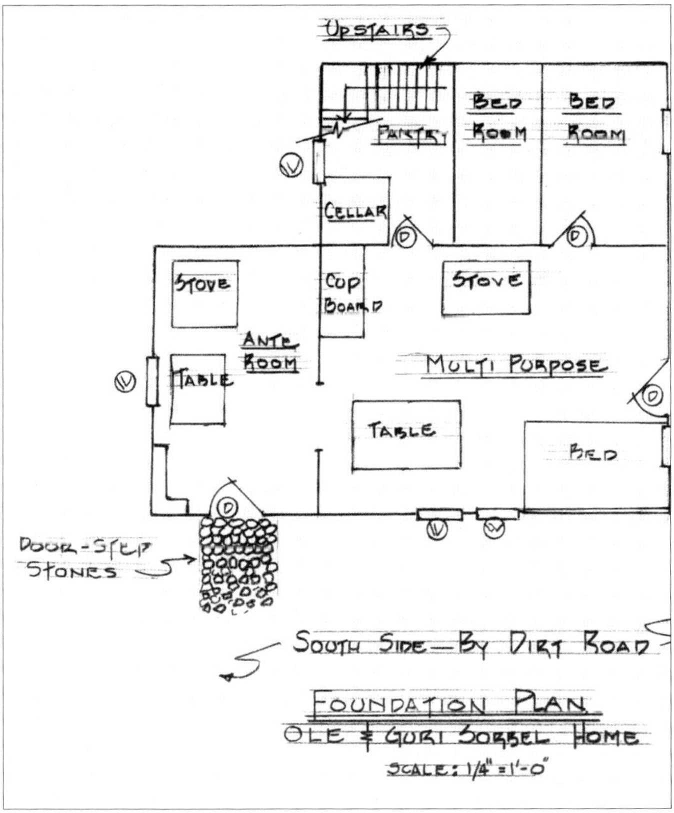

Sorbel home floor plan. *Drafted from original sketch by author.*

This log cabin was erected about 1856 and stood until the mid-1930s. *Courtesy of* From Norway to Home.

The cabin had one large room with a divider at the end to make two bedrooms. A lean-to was added on the west side, and a sleeping loft was built up above. It was cold in the loft in the winter and hot and full of mosquitoes in the summer. The cabin was an improvement over many homes, as it had a chimney and a cookstove.

This cabin built with black walnut logs served the Sorbels until it was torn down in 1930. (Ole's son Asle would die in that same year in a distant Dakota town.) The logs have been preserved as building material for the Nora Unitarian Church/Museum in rural Hanska, which exists to the present day.

One connection to this cabin is that Robert Sorbel's father, Henry, was born in it. (Robert Sorbel is husband to memoir writer Jan Sorbel.) Asle Oscar Sorbel's brother Ole Jr. was Henry's father. Asle Oscar Sorbel was the uncle of Henry and the great-uncle to Robert Sorbel.

The Linden area was virgin prairie when Ole and Guri arrived. An old-time settler wrote, reminiscent of Ole Rølvaag descriptions of the countryside, "I am standing on the highest hill by Lake Hanska and except for this brushy hill and the woods over by Linden Lake, there is nothing but great plains stretching as far as the eye can see. In the dim horizon, it was like an ocean, with green waves of grass."

Logs from Ole and Guri Sorbel home repurposed to build the Nora Museum near Hanska, Minnesota. *Courtesy SR Photography, St. James, Minnesota.*

The Linden land belonged to the Sioux Indian Nation. The Linden area became the property of the United States by the signing of the Treaty of Traverse des Sioux on July 23, 1851. The land was surveyed in 1855, and the new township of Linden was so named because of all the linden trees around the adjoining lake. The lake was also called Linden Lake.

While the linden trees growing fifty to one hundred feet high offered ideal shade with their attractive form and dark green foliage, little did Ole and Guri dream that this sacred pastoral scene, and their mellow farm life, would one day be interrupted by whizzing bullets and gun blasts.

But for now—all was serene.

To encourage settlers, the government rewarded citizens who had served in the armed services between 1776 and 1855 with so many acres of land per year of service.

This piece of ground that Ole and Guri settled on had been given in 1858 to Private William R. Lowry for serving in the Georgia War, also sometimes called the Seminole Wars, which took place from 1816 to 1858. The land grants were called "county patents." Most of the time, the southern soldiers who were given these bounty patents wouldn't live up north, even if the land was given to them. Speculators went around and bought these land grant papers for small amounts of money, came up North and sold them for big profits to settlers who wanted the land. Sometimes these bounty papers were saved, like money in the bank, and long after the original soldier had died, it was given to the heirs, who would sell them. The title to the land shows that Lowery completed the "Bounty Patent transaction on April 10, 1862. It is signed by Abraham Lincoln and is recorded in the New Ulm courthouse."

Lowery's piece of land was 120 acres. The Bounty Land Claim form shows that Private Lowery received the acreage after serving only three months—from June to September of 1836. Ole purchased, according to the transaction document, 90 and 30/100ths of an acre. The odd figure appeared because the lake shore on one side of the farm made the measurements uneven.

As the Norwegian settlers were establishing farms, homes and families in the new country, they recognized their need to give thanks for the bounty they were enjoying. Their connection from the land to God, from the creation to the Creator, burst forth in a "Takk for Sist" and mange takk. "Many, many thanks" (translation) led to a desire for worship. With gratitude, they envisioned a place for the community to gather and worship.

On July 6, 1859 (the year Asle Oscar Sorbel was born), the Sorbels and twelve other families met with a minister from Winona, Minnesota, by the name of Reverend Frederickson to organize a Lutheran congregation. The thirteen charter families were:

Jens P. Harbo
Knudt H. Helling Sr.
Tore Olson Kirkebon
Endre C. Levig
Torsten C. Levig
Ever Nelson
Ole Thordson Omsrud
Helge Palma
Anders Olson Skurleik
Ole Sorbel
Gunnar Paulson
Peder Thormodson
Torgrim Torgrimson

After organizing as a Lutheran congregation, the next step they needed was a place to build a church structure and cemetery. How did the Linden people fare?

> *A struggle developed over where the church and cemetery were to be located with several locations proposed and insisted on.... Knudt H. Helling Sr. came forward and offered a compromise—if they could come to an agreement, two acres could be selected somewhere on his farm. His compromise offer was accepted for a price of $11.00. The Linden Lutheran Cemetery was dedicated and consecrated as the burial grounds for the Linden Lutheran Congregation on the 12th of July 1867.*[1]

Despite arguments and disagreements, many simply agreed to disagree and get along.

The children "read" for the minister. This is what confirmation instruction was called at the time. The children met in homes and after the lessons would be served a delicious lunch so that all the students got a sample of the cooking in the neighborhood. Reverend L.E. Green, who served from 1873 to 1907, confirmed Asle Oscar and his siblings.

Asle confirmed his baptism into Christ on May 3, 1874. Asle's siblings followed suit: Gunnil on October 28, 1877; Sigri (Siri) on November 19, 1879; Lisa on September 30, 1883; Olette on November 20, 1887; and brother Martin on September 24, 1881.

Linden Lutheran Church of Hanska prospered and maintained a viable and lively ministry for devout and loyal settlers, as well as their descendants, for 151 years, closing in 2010.

The first school in the territory was taught in the home of Peter Thormodson with twenty-six students. The teacher was Charles Mullen. Linden was the first of the Brown County schools to be taught by a man. In the spring of 1862, a log school was built for both the Linden and Lake Hanska townships to use. This became district no. 7. The Sorbels attended this school even though the school term was only two to three months long, as the children were needed to help with the farm work during the planting, growing and harvest seasons.

In 1861, the area was devastated by prairie fires. Many people lost their homes. But the Sorbels were spared.

In 1862, the Sioux Indian uprising occurred. J.S. Helling tells of the only killing in the Hanska area during this war:

> *A bachelor, named J. Armstrong lived across the lake from the Sorbel's. On the day of the Indian attack, neighbors heard shooting coming from the direction of Mr. Armstrong's place. They were afraid of running into a band of Indians and so did not go to investigate until the next day. When*

they got to the Armstrong home, he was not to be found but after some searching, his body was located where it had been hidden under a brush pile on Anton Ouren's place, near the barn. This was close to the lake and in the wet earth were tracks of three warriors. The arrow in Mr. Arrnstrong's back was pulled out and tossed into the lake. Then the men followed the Indian's trail. The trail led up to where the Unitarian cemetery is now and after finding a bloody moccasin, indicating that Armstrong had at least wounded one of them, the chase stopped.

Records show that Ole Sorbel bought 4 acres of land from the small plots in the SW section 29 from the estate of James Armstrong, February 11 in 1864.

Life for the early pioneer settlers at Linden had its challenges. They survived Indian uprisings, prairie fires, drought, locusts and quarrels. Yet they persevered.

And then it happened, on a most unexpected, unforgettable raucous September day in 1876.

1
MAYHEM NINETY MILES EAST

Violent fires soon burn out themselves, small showers last long, but sudden storms are short; he tires betimes that spurs too fast.

—William Shakespeare in Richard II

September 21, 1876, started as an ordinary, sleepy day, but Asle Oscar Sorbel came in contact with four strangers who would change his life forever. That day, Asle, a second-generation Norwegian lad, and four desperate men crossed paths at Ole and Guri Sorbel's farm, a stone's throw from Linden Lake, north and west of Madelia, Minnesota.

The events that led up to Asle's life-changing story began one Thursday two weeks earlier, on September 7, 1876, ninety miles east of the Sorbel farm.

That day, around 2:00 p.m., the Jesse James/Younger brothers' outlaw gang decided to do a "little banking" in the prosperous and somnolent town of Northfield, Minnesota. The town motto, "Cows, Colleges and Contentment," reflected the sunny climate of the day.

Eight men leisurely cased the town most of that morning. They eyed and then patronized their target, casually getting change while checking the clock at the First National Bank on Division Street.

The First National Bank was an appealing target. There was plenty of loot to be acquired. The farmers had done well. Wealth was evident. Another motivation for doing a little banking was that Adelbert Ames possessed a large investment in the bank. Ames was a northerner, a Union Civil War

First National Bank of Northfield, Minnesota. *Courtesy of the Northfield Historical Society, Northfield, Minnesota.*

Interior First National Bank view, 1876. *Courtesy of the Northfield Historical Society.*

general and the son-in-law of the hated Union general Benjamin Butler. The southern outlaws smelled vengeance. But they also reeked raw greed.

The men, with exceptionally fine horses and McCellan saddlery to match, pretended to be land speculators and livestock buyers. Druggist George Bates recalled later seeing them ride into town; he said he had never seen "nobler looking fellows." "He had observed that the strangers had a 'reckless, bold swagger about them that seemed to indicate that they would be rough and dangerous fellows to handle.'"[1]

Several townspeople, some former Civil War veterans, thought the strangers' rather arrogant confidence and exceptional horses displayed the look of a "guerrilla raid." One of them even shouted, "It's a St. Albans raid!" (On October 19, 1864, at St. Albans, Vermont, the northernmost site of the war, twenty-one Confederate guerrilla soldiers left Canadian territory, raced into Union territory, attacked and robbed a bank in an effort to help fund the Southern cause. They got their money, killed a local citizen and escaped.)

Hardware store owner J.S. Allen became suspicious. These striking, duster-dressed strangers in town seemed out of place. Twenty-two-year-old Henry Wheeler eyed them with curiosity. An uncomfortable feeling welled up inside of him as he sat near his father's drugstore, Wheeler and Blackman Drug.

Then came kairos—time to act! Jesse James, Bill Chadwell and Jim Younger positioned themselves quietly on Mill Square, ensuring an escape route over the bridge spanning the Cannon River. Cole Younger and Clell Miller had posted themselves on Division Street near the bank. Frank James, Bob Younger and Charlie Pitts would enter the bank, demand to open the vault and steal what was estimated to be $15,000 to $25,000.

Suddenly, outside the bank, the loud crack of .44 Smith & Wesson revolvers split the air. The outlaws blasted away with their .44 Navy Colts and .45-caliber single-action army pistols, cursing and shouting at everyone on Mill Square and Division Street. "Get off the streets you s-o-bs!"

At first, the Northfield citizens presumed the whooping, the hollering and the pistol shots in the air belied a simple promotional stunt. A patient in dentist Dr. Whiting's office suggested there was to be an Indian show that evening and the ruckus was advertising the event. Dr. Whiting immediately went out to the stairs to check.

Other Northfield citizens thought there was to be a circus in town. Still others expected and assumed the ruckus advertised that evening's entertainment. The show on deck promised to feature "The Great Professor

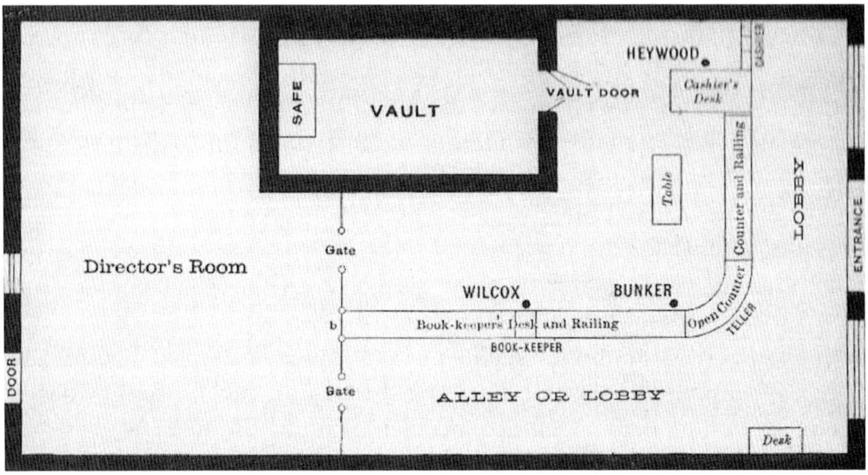

Floor plan of the First National Bank. *Courtesy of the Northfield Historical Society.*

Lingard," an Australian illusionist. The Northfield residents were promised they would gasp and marvel at two gas balloons ascending high into the air, the aerostats named "Tilden and Hayes [the Democratic and Republican candidates for president]."[2]

It would be an extravaganza. Balloons, the Great Professor Lingard and a magic/illusion show, coming to Northfield!

But this was no show before the show. The mayhem was for real.

The day, which began quietly, like after a morning rain, would end up deadly—an angry tornado. Frank, Bob and Clell strode into the First National Bank of Northfield—trusting the other outlaws standing watch outside. But the plan to rob the bank and ride away scot-free never happened. When hardware owner J.S. Allen suspected trouble, he was accosted by Clell Miller at the bank door and ran away shouting, "Get your guns boys they're robbing the bank."[3]

A few Northfield citizens owned guns but normally used them for hunting prairie chickens. Much to the outlaws' surprise, they shot back—a lot of them shot back.

C.E. Bates grabbed a shotgun, pointed at one of the outlaws and jerked the trigger, but the gun failed to fire. A handy revolver also failed to fire. It was unloaded, so Bates pretended to fire. Trying to fool the bandits, he apparently only endangered himself. Northfield's town marshal, Elias Hobbs, though unarmed, courageously (or foolishly) hurled rocks at the robbers. Others with newfound bravado lobbed any projectile they could grab.

All eight outlaws—Jesse and Frank James, Cole, Jim and Bob Younger, Charlie Pitts, Clell Miller and Bill Chadwell—fired, sending bullets into the air and at any and all who would resist. Blasting, yelling, cursing, they intimidated every bystanders who stood in their way. Frank, Bob and Charlie raced into the bank, revolvers cocked, "Put up your hands and keep 'em up or I'll kill you," barked Bob.

Acting cashier for the day Joseph Heywood either resisted too much or reacted too slowly when they shouted, "Open that safe…and be quick about it or I'll blow your head off."[4] A rap on the head by Frank's revolver butt sent Heywood to the floor, bleeding yet conscious. Joseph Heywood was the city treasurer and also treasurer of the newly formed Carleton College. A robbery of Carleton College's meager funds in the bank vault would bankrupt the nascent college. The bankers, Alonzo Bunker and assistant bookkeeper Frank Wilcox, outsmarted the gang by telling them there was a time lock on the safe, even though it was actually unlocked in the open vault. Next, the outlaws fired a slug at Alonzo Bunker, the bank's teller, hitting him in the shoulder as he dashed out the back door down the alley. The shot barely missed his would-be-deadly subclavian artery.

Frank Wilcox, the assistant bookkeeper, flew out the back door and across the alley to Anselm Manning's hardware store. Then, in the melee, Joseph Heywood, reluctant and too slow to cooperate, took a bullet to the left

Bank shootout. *Courtesy of the Denver Public Library, C364.D714oud, interior scene of bank robbery from* The Complete and Authentic History of the Lives of Frank and Jesse James and Their Robber Companions, including Quantrill and His Noted Guerrillas, the Greatest Bandits the World Has Ever Known, *by Jay Donald, published by Douglas Brothers, Philadelphia, PA, 1882.*

Right: Photo of Joseph Lee Heywood, the assistant acting cashier the day of the robbery. Heywood was also the city treasurer as well as the treasurer of the newly formed Carleton College. He served in the bank with bookkeeper Frank J. Wilcox and teller Alonzo E. Bunker. Suddenly, three strangers burst into the room. The perpetrators—some authorities claim it was Jesse James, Frank James and Charlie Pitts—demanded the money. In the melee, Bunker was shot in the shoulder as he ran out the back door. Heywood was not so lucky. He was shot and killed. The prevailing belief is that Frank James shot the resisting and unlucky banker Heywood. *Courtesy of the Northfield Historical Society.*

Below: Christdala Church, later called by some historians the "Church that Jesse Built." More accurately, historians might call the Christdala Church the "Church that Jesse James caused, by the shooting death of Nicolaus Gustafson." *Courtesy of the Rice County Historical Society Collection.*

temple. Heywood prevented another St. Albans by his heroic action, but with his blood oozing on the bank floor, he lost his life.

Cole Younger, appointed guardian of the street for the getaway, hollered at a strolling Swedish immigrant named Nicolaus Gustafson, "Get off the streets or you'll be killed." Gustafson had ridden into town that morning with Peter Youngquist, who owned the only span of mules in the Swedish community nearby. Historians guess that Gustafson either ignored the warning or did not understand the command. Some think he was drunk, though that has been disputed. Gustafson did not leave the street. Did Cole Younger lower his revolver and pull the trigger? Or was Gustafson shot in the crossfire? It is unknown. However, seriously wounded, he would die a few days later in the Northfield Norwegian Hospital.

As an aside, fast-forward to a year later. Christdala Evangelical Swedish Church would be founded in 1877 and built two miles west of Millersburg by Nicolaus Gustafson's brother Peter Gustafson and Peter Youngquist.

This is near where Cole, Jim, Clell and Pitts had lodged the night before the robbery attempt and where the outlaws would soon speedily pass after the shootout. A historical plague at this site commemorates the Northfield fiasco and particularly Nicolaus Gustafson's innocent and unfortunate role.

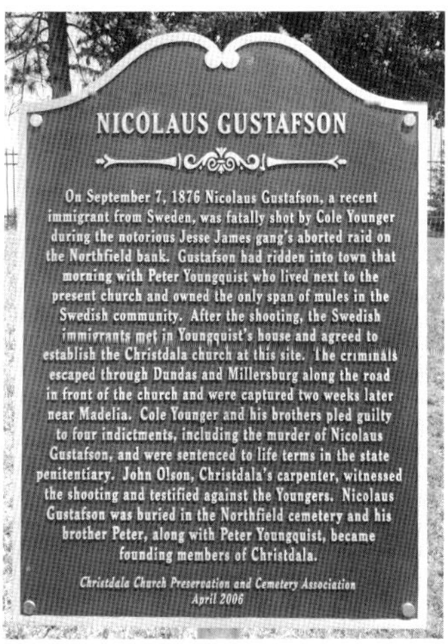

Historic Gustafson Memorial Plaque located near the Christdala Evangelical Swedish Lutheran Church, eleven miles west of Northfield. Nicolaus Gusfason was the Swedish immigrant who was mortally wounded in Northfield in the midst of the Younger-James bank robbery fiasco. *Courtesy of the Rice County Historical Society.*

The mayhem in First National Bank turned into a bust. The gang miscalculated the "mild-mannered Minnesotans." Peace-loving and law-abiding, yes. Passive citizens they were not. "Get your guns, robbers, robbers, they're robbing our bank!"[5] Then all h—— broke loose!

Citizen Elias Stacy fired a fowling gun at Clell Miller and hit him in the face with birdshot as he mounted his horse.

Medical student Henry Wheeler, home on vacation from his studies at the University of Michigan, grabbed a .52-caliber Smith carbine and four cartridges. He had been sitting near the bank. He flew up the stairs to the second floor of the Dampier House hotel across the street from the bank. He began firing. He hit Clell Miller, tumbling

Engraving from a contemporary woodcut from Jay Lemon's *The Northfield Tragedy, 1876* of the shootout on Division Street. *Courtesy of the Northfield Historical Society.*

Clell from his horse and severing his subclavian artery. Not as lucky as Alonzo Bunker, Clell Miller bled to death on the spot.

Anselm Manning, the other hardware store owner, pulled out a Remington rolling block rifle from his store window. He shot and killed Bob Younger's horse. Then he shot and killed Bill Chadwell from nearly seventy yards away. Next, he hit Cole Younger in the hip. Jim was struck and wounded in the shoulder. A bullet smashed Frank James's right thigh. Everyone was hit and bleeding, except Jesse James and Charlie Pitts.

The robbery attempt turned into a rout. Cole Younger yelled to the three still in the bank, "For God's sake come out. They're shooting us all to pieces."

The remaining six outlaws headed for their mounts. Six of the eight rode out on five horses, bullets whistling all around. They headed for the Big Woods of Minnesota to escape and to hide.

The tally: The Northfield mayhem lasted seven to ten minutes. The grain sack for the money was rendered useless, except for about $26.70 in coin and scrip.[6]

Three men were dead—Joseph Heywood, the cashier, and Bill Chadwell and Clell Miller, outlaws—with Nicolaus Gustafson mortally wounded.

During the fury, ninety miles away to the west, the rains began to pelt gently on fields, farms and Linden Lake in Brown County. The Ole Sorbels and son Asle Oscar, unaware of the mayhem to the east, continued to go about cultivating, haying and harvesting, pursuing a living—peacefully and productively—but not for long.

2

TRANQUILITY AT OLE'S FARM—DRAMA IN THE BIG WOODS

AND THE TWO THAT GOT AWAY

He can run, but he can't hide.
—Joe Louis before his heavyweight fight with Billy Conn, 1948

Typically, from midsummer to late September, grain harvests produced bountiful crops in Watonwan* County. Oats, wheat, rye, barley and corn luckily sidestepped capricious weather tantrums—drought, hail, wind and locusts—and escaped to safe storage places in farmers' barns and granary bins. Haying the fields and meadows produced stacks of prairie hay for the winter. Daily livestock chores demanded attention from the barnyard—milking, feeding, slopping pigs and picking eggs. Soon an early frost would perform an orchestration of colors. Everywhere one would see the magic of artists deftly touching thousands of leaves. Painted golden yellow, orange and red, the foliage emblazoned the countryside around Linden Lake. Groves of lindens and stands of black walnut, ash and oak sheltered all who lingered in their shade. The lake itself, asleep and waveless, absorbed the warm rays of the sun. Neighbors chatted unhurriedly. A meadow lark chirped to its now nearly grown chicks.

Typically, this pastoral scene prevailed—but this year?

---

* *Watonwan* is a Native American word for "place of many fish" or "fish bait."

Ole's family, along with son Asle, went about their chores and farm duties while six outlaws on five horses were last seen riding west, recklessly fast, out of Northfield, Minnesota. They had to get away—and get away fast.

Bob Younger's handsome bay horse lay dead on Division Street—a target of Northfield hardware store owner Anselm Manning's Remington rifle slug. The six riders on five horses rode hard, feeling the hot breath of determined, hastily organized posse/vigilantes on their necks.

The three-mile ride southwest to Dandas in Rice County did not take very long. It was the only spot to cross the Canon River.

Unfortunately for them, before they left Northfield, the gang had not wrecked the equipment at the telegraph office as planned, nor were they able to cut the telegraph wires. Already word of the bank robbery attempt was clicking fast down the wires from town to town.

The luckless gang fled desperately, but they must stop. Near the Canon River bridge, they cleansed their wounds. Jim had received four wounds in Northfield; Cole, eleven; Frank had a leg wound; and Bob's shattered elbow lay cradled in a bloody sling. Outlaws Bill Chadwell and Clell Miller lay back in the streets, dead. Luckily, Charlie Pitts and Jesse James had escaped the firestorm unscathed, at least for the present.

Just before entering Dundas, they stopped at Robert Donaldson's farm and asked for a pail of water for rinsing Bob Younger's broken, bleeding elbow.[1]

Passing beyond Dundas, the gang met a hired hand driving a spring wagon hauling hoop poles with a team of horses. (Other sources indicate only one horse was involved.) Quickly Bob dismounted from Cole's steed and commandeered his own horse, but it was a workhorse, no racing stallion. The owner, Phillip Empey, was away. The hapless hired hand hiked back to town.[2]

Ole Sorbel, Norwegian immigrant and now settler and steward of a piece of Minnesota soil, no doubt felt like the immigrant, Per Hansa, in Ole Rølvaag's *Giants in the Earth*:

> *Once more Per Hansa's heart filled with a deep sense of peace and contentment as he realized how matters were being smoothed out for him. They seemed to move of their own accord, but he knew better.... Was he really to own it? Was it really to become his possession, this big stretch of fine land that spread here before him? Was he really to have his friends for neighbors, both to the north and to the south—folks who cared for him and wanted to help him out in every way?*[3]

Mother Guri Sorbel, reflected, not unlike Beret in Rølvaag's novel, "who sat down and let her gaze wander aimlessly around....In a certain sense, she had to admit to herself, it was lovely up here. The broad expanse stretching away endlessly in every direction, seemed almost like ocean—especially now, when darkness was falling. It reminded her strongly of the sea, and yet it was very different."[4]

It was late September 1876, and the skies of Watonwan County spawned threatening cloud banks in the west. Soon torrents of bone-chilling rain would muddy the Sorbel farmland and blanket the earth all the way from Madelia to Mankato to Dundas to Northfield, Minnesota.

Back in Northfield, a posse of sorts hurriedly formed. It included the mayor, a dozen or so excited townsfolk and Carleton College graduate and medical student Henry Mason Wheeler. (Other sources, such as John Koblas's *Minnesota Grit* and Wayne Fanebust's *Chasing Frank and Jesse James*, indicate that Dr. Wheeler stayed in Northfield and dealt with the two outlaw corpses destined to become celebrity cadavers.)

Soon dozens more men turned out to hunt the outlaws. Farmers and townspeople grabbed their fowling pieces, rifles and pistols, jumped into wagons and mounted saddle horses. Unbeknownst to the gang, they would gather the largest manhunt in the history of the country. Over one thousand law enforcers, common folks and reward seekers would eventually hunt the hunted.

By this time, about two hours after the rout in Northfield, the gang had gone another six plus miles, galloping through Millersburg, stopping at Shieldsville. Different narratives tell what happened in Shieldsville.

In his book *Cole Younger: The Last of the Great Outlaws*, Homer Croy recounts the gang stopping at a small hotel (probably the Cushman Hotel) to get something to eat. There the gang saw, leaning against the porch railing, a line of rifles and muskets. The Faribault posse was inside eating. The gang simply slipped away.[5]

In *Outlaw Youngers: A Confederate Brotherhood*, Marley Brant relates how Bob fainted and fell off his horse. An older man saw the faint and fall and asked about what just happened. Jesse James thought quickly as he helped Bob back on his horse, saying, "We're going to hang that damn cuss," explaining that Bob was a captured horse thief.[6]

Wayne Fanebust's perspective, from newspaper resources, pictures the scene differently. Apparently, the outlaw hunters, a squad of Faribault men, were having a few drinks at Joseph Hagerty's store and saloon. They had left their guns with their horses outside. After washing their wounds, the gang faced the "happy" posse who had emerged, threatened them with their revolvers and then shot up the water pump before leaving town.[7]

Cole Younger in his *The Story of Cole Younger by Himself* remembered that the squad of men—S.T. Seaman, J. McCann and two Lev brothers from Shieldsview plus others—overtook the gang and exchanged shots in a ravine, but without any serious effect on either side, although Cole was struck on his crazy bone by a spent bullet.[8]

The rain would continue on and off for the next two weeks from Shieldsville to Madelia to the Sorbel farm near Linden Lake. At the Sorbel farm, the fields and area roads yielding to the menacing clouds became drenched by the downpour, making the simplest farm work challenging, aggravating, but manageable. (Fast-forward nine days, a mud-plastered Asle Sorbel would ride into Madelia after his old workhorse had slipped and fallen on that soaked and muddy road.)

Meanwhile, St. Paul detective John B. Bresette, Minneapolis detective Michael Hoy, old Civil War veterans, Rice County sheriff Ara Barton and other wannabe vigilantes of all sorts joined the hunt near Faribault. The gang had already slipped into the Big Woods of Minnesota to hide. Determined, desperate they would escape. The Big Woods enveloped a vast forest of two million acres interspersed with meadows, marshes with muddy bottoms and large tracts of old-growth woods. Roads were scarce, if they existed at all. The friendly though challenging woods were full of thickets and ravines. Lakes, streams and boggy swamps along with the incessant rain obliterated tracks and other signs, helping hide the hunted.

In the temporary safety of the woods, the battered gang assessed their wounds. Bob continued to bleed from his now swollen arm as he developed a fever from the infection. Jim's shoulder, causing stabbing pain, also became infected. Cole tied his bleeding thigh tightly and relied on a quickly fashioned walking cane. Frank suffered from a bullet wound to his leg. At Kilkenny, the fugitives stopped for the night at the Dan and Jane Walsh farm. They slept in the barn and paid the couple for their lodging when they left.[9]

The fleeing gang raced through Morristown and into LeSeur County. Their horses, lathered white with sweat, would soon be abandoned near German Lake.

In the Big Woods, at this point, they were surrounded by nearly two hundred hunters.

The outlaws pushed on beyond Waterville and Elysian. Then on to Okaman, they passed near Madison Lake. A posse waited for them at Eagle

Lake, ready to begin the chase. At Marysburg the now horseless six-some continued on foot.

On September 13, eight days after the raid, the six outlaws, now three miles north of Mankato, appeared at the Henry Shaubert farm. There they came upon a thirty-three-year-old farmhand named Thomas Jefferson Dunning. They demanded that Dunning show them the way to Mankato. First, they learned about the nature of the area, the roads or any skiffs on the Minnesota river from him. After several hours of off-and-on interrogation, the outlaws knew they had a problem. Dunning would be able to identify the bandits, so they considered tying him to a tree or killing him. Then one of the outlaws said loudly so Dunning would hear him, "Let's shoot the s-o-b." After a heated discussion, the gang released Dunning and let him go and thereby took their chances.

Dunning pondered what to do. Worried sick about threats, he nonetheless ran to his employer, Henry Shaubert, and told him what had happened. Shaubert immediately dashed to the authorities and sounded the alarm.[10]

On September 14, the outlaws crossed the Blue Earth River on the railroad tracks near Mankato. It was déjà vu for Cole, as he had cased the town on September 2 and particularly the First National Bank on Front Street in Mankato before the Northfield raid. (After his parole, Cole would visit the town again.)

As the gang continued on the run, they eluded Detective Michael Hoy, posted guards and strategically positioned reward-hungry citizens.

Governor J.S. Pillsbury issued a reward proclamation: "A reward of $1,500 was promised by the state for the capture, dead or alive, of the men who committed the raid, and afterwards escaped, on the bank of Northfield on September 7, 1876, or a proportionate amount for any one of them captured."[11]

Pickets surrounding the area had been set up by General Edmund Pope, headquartered at Eagle Lake. According to a Mankato newspaper, General Pope's impeccable war record made him the right man for the job. "General Pope's war record is a particularly brilliant one. There were few harder fighters or more determined campaigners than he. Not knowing the meaning of fear, he never shirked a duty, no matter how arduous and chose the most dangerous assignments."[12] After General Pope was called to coordinate the search efforts, he quickly declared, "We'll soon get them."

At Lake Crystal, the James brothers separated from the rest of the gang. Was the leave-taking planned? Was it amicable? Was the separation unintended or happened by chance? In one of his many later prison discussions, Cole

Younger remarked, "We parted in peace." (Wayne Fanebust details the subsequent escape of Jesse and Frank James in his detailed and fascinating book *Chasing Frank and Jesse James* from 2018.)

But now could the gang break through Pope's picket lines? It was agreed that the James brothers should go ahead and reconnoiter in an attempt to locate the pickets. "A large black horse was taken from the farm of John Vincent…east of Lake Crystal…and about midnight the two men on one stolen horse, attempted to cross a picket line on the road near the outlet of Loon Lake."[13]

> *The area was well guarded but most of the guards had fallen asleep on some straw scattered along the road, leaving one young Welsh man, Richard Roberts, awake, alert, standing near the bridge. He was on guard when the (black) horse quietly approached. He fired in the dark spooking the horse causing it to flinch to the side.*
>
> *The brothers suddenly found themselves on the ground with their horse running away.*
>
> *They crawled away in the dark woods while the black horse galloped away.*[14]

The black horse running off ended up as a merciful decoy. The picket guards were totally distracted. The James boys got away. "But again the fugitives escaped, not so much by virtue of their own cunning as through favorable accidents and the inefficiency of the guards on duty."[15]

"On foot, Frank and Jesse came upon a farm near Garden City owned by a man named Seymour in whose stable were two fine gray horses. The horses belonged to a Methodist minister named George Rockwood. After a scuffle with the minister, the James raced away, traveling seventy five miles in one day."[16]

Eventually, by deception, avoiding and dodging the posses of Sheriff Ara Barton of Fairbault County, Detective Mike Hoy and Sheriff Dill of Winona County and changing stolen horses on the way, the James boys headed for Dakota Territory.

They reached the Palisades near Garretson, South Dakota. With a posse hell-bent on capture or kill, Jesse soared into myth and legend by supposedly spurring his mount and jumping recklessly over Devil's Gulch Chasm.

This leap over the ravine above Split Rock Creek, flanked by quartzite rock walls, aptly called Devil's Gulch, excites storytellers to the present day, even though the twenty-foot leap was virtually impossible. The tale does not explain what happened to Frank, nor does it explain how or why only Jesse

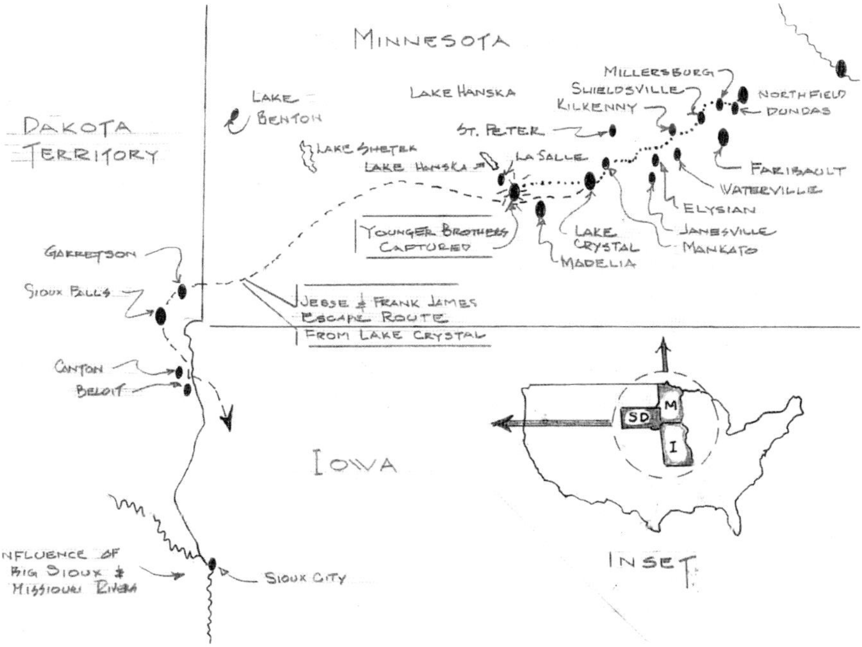

Map of escape route. *Sketch by author.*

leaped over the chasm. It appears Jesse and Frank actually rode several miles to the south. Jesse James history aficionados also wonder how would it be possible that the two stolen iron-gray mares, by this time totally exhausted, had such leaping energy?

There is no dispute that the great escape of the James brothers succeeded. A hundred stories both fact and fiction followed their trails. A hundred more wait to be discovered and told.

One of the latest stories, as this account goes to press, features a historic log cabin that has been physically moved from the Humphrey Ranch south and west of Custer, South Dakota, to the 1881 Courthouse Museum site in Custer. Seth Bullock, frontiersman, sheriff, and U.S. marshal who lived in Deadwood, and Theodore Roosevelt stayed at this wayside inn, as did Jesse James at some time during his outlaw career. Toots Schriner verifies these stories as told to her by her grandmother of the then Schriner Ranch. (For update, see Director Jeanne Kirkpatrick of the 1881 Courthouse Museum.)

Meanwhile, as rain pelted the Watonwan River, northwest of Madelia, Minnesota, the Ole Sorbel family milked, fed livestock and cleaned the barnyard. The countryside, peaceful with gentle rain, bathed the settlers'

Custer Log Cabin Inn on the Schriner Ranch southwest of Custer, South Dakota. Theodore Roosevelt, Deadwood sheriff and U.S. marshal Seth Bullock and Jesse James were remembered as guests. Custer and Schriner ranch resident Toots Schriner remembered her grandmother telling her that Jesse James stayed in this cabin for a while. *Courtesy of Bradley J. Boner.*

Log Cabin Inn on the Deadwood stage trail from the Schriner Ranch moved in 2020 to a new site near the 1881 Courthouse Museum in Custer. *Courtesy of 1881 Courthouse Museum Director Jeanne Kirkpatrick.*

fields and pastures. Ole Sorbel's homesteaded land mirrored Rølvaag's description of Hans Olsa's:

> *The third quarter-section which Hans Olsa owned lay near the creek, north of Solums. This he had fenced in and was using as a pasture for a large herd. During the summer he did not need to look after the cattle at all, except to give them salt; the grass was plentiful up north and they could drink at the creek. The preceding year the herd had pastured there until late in the fall. This year he had hauled over all the straw he could spare, and had bought more where he could find it.*[17]

Ole, too, was pleased that his pastures, now drinking in the rain, would provide plenty for his herd and crops. It was an idyllic time. But peaceful breezes and calm waters at Linden Lake were not to last.

Four desperate strangers emerging from the big woods would stir up a tornado that Madelia, its citizens and history would not soon forget.

3
ASLE'S "PAUL REVERE" RIDE

Ride fast, ride strong, be nimble, be quick, the devil's hot breath is on your neck.
—AKF

Most contemporary students of poetry have read and perhaps memorized Henry Wadsworth Longfellow's version of this event in the classic poem "Paul Revere's Ride."

Whether Asle Oscar Sorbel had exposure to the story and subsequent poetry of the ride of Paul Revere in school or was even aware of this legendary event in early American Revolutionary War history is unknown. Nonetheless, Madelia citizens, proud and inspired by Asle's cool and courageous actions that day, September 21, 1876, would proudly dub him and his legacy, the "Paul Revere of Watonwan County."

The wild chase through the Big Woods reached high intensity. Posses, vigilantes, detectives, sheriffs, farmers and townsfolk picked up arms and joined the chase. The persistent rain tortured both the hunters and the hunted.

When the news of the Northfield raid reached Mankato, Civil War hero General Edmund Mann Pope was placed in charge to coordinate the search efforts. Assuming command, he left his farm produce and machinery business in Mankato and set up headquarters at Eagle Lake. Then he relocated his headquarters to Lake Crystal, fourteen miles southwest of Mankato. By the early evening of Thursday, September 14, he had set up a new picket line with hundreds of men that stretched in a twelve-mile

Midnight Ride of Paul Revere. Sketch by author.

semicircle. But ten men supposedly assigned to guard a bridge over a small creek fell asleep.

> *At midnight ten guards snored away, as two riders on one horse galloped by. Frank and Jesse spurred a recently stolen horse at break neck speed. One guard, Richard Roberts, heard the hoof beats in the sand, and cried out "Halt! Who are you fellows?" The James boys raced on. Roberts raised his gun and fired. The horse jumped and its riders tumbled to the ground. The James boys rebounded and scattered to a cornfield.*[1]

At daylight, Detective Michael Hoy from Minneapolis and his squad arrived at Lake Crystal. They received the news from an anxious Baptist minister named Joseph Rockwood, who reported that his team of iron-gray mares had been stolen. The horses were taken from a farm three miles to the south at approximately at 3:00 am.

Reverend Rockwood had good reason to be upset, because his large mares were considered the best team in Blue Earth County.[2] (Other sources say it was a Methodist elder whose name was George Rockwood.)

By this time, Frank and Jesse James had separated from the Youngers near Lake Crystal, Minnesota. They raced on their way to Dakota Territory, no longer encumbered by the Youngers and Charlie Pitts. Bob had slowed up the escape because of his serious, painful and bleeding wound.

Astride two strong mounts, Frank and Jesse James moved quickly, galloping ahead of pursuing posses and vigilante groups. Many sightings of the fleeting James brothers kept the telegraph operators buzzing—even though the two desperadoes had, in fact, escaped. (As mentioned in chapter 3, many both true and fictional sightings are chronicled in Wayne Fanebust's 2018 book *Chasing Frank and Jesse James*.)

Detective Hoy and his party continued searching along the tracks of the Sioux City Railroad. Then they saw a light blue smoke rising out of the brush about ten rods from the tracks. Rather than encircle the robbers and send a man for additional help, Hoy's eager men dashed blindly into the woods, driving the fleeing bandits up a bluff known as Pigeon Hill.[3]

The foursome got away. Detective Michel Hoy and his men found a camping area where the outlaws had left some green corn and prepared chickens, which had been obviously stolen. The posse also found two bridles, a linen duster, a handkerchief covered with bloodstains and parts of a bloody shirt. The detective got close but not close enough. The outlaws pushed on through the swampland seven miles north of Madelia.

Word had gotten to Madelia by telegraph that the robbers were on the loose and possibly headed that way. The Youngers and Charlie Pitts had been on foot for several days. Minnesota had become their living hell. The rain and cold continued to sap their strength, making their escape a terrible ordeal. Cole Younger would say later that they were intent on stealing some good horses at a farm as they trudged north and then west of Mankato, but they were unsuccessful. They had left the Big Woods. Now they were in open prairie land and with fewer places to hide. Night must be their cover and protector. Cole carried a cane he now used for walking. Bob's blasted broken elbow in a sling resisted straightening. He could not use his fingers.

Cole remembered a little village of eight hundred or so people southwest of Mankato he had visited on the way to Northfield. It was Madelia, Minnesota. He somewhat knew the area since he had been there before. "But the ragtag band, their various wounds seeping blood and pus, made little progress, camping in one patch of timber for two nights and another near Lake Linden for three."[4]

One Madelia resident was not that surprised at the pending appearance of the gang. He was Colonel Thomas Lent Vought, a business owner in town. Colonel Vought, who was living in Bryce Prairie, Wisconsin, when the Civil War broke out, served in the Fourteenth Wisconsin Regiment for the entire campaign. After he retired, in 1866, he traveled to Madelia, Minnesota, where he began farming and raising stock. He also opened a stagecoach line. When the railroad appropriated his business as a stagecoach line operator, he purchased a hotel called the Flanders House.

About a month earlier, around August 23, 1876, "two men had stopped by the Flanders House and registered as J.C. King and Jack Ward. They arrived in the middle of the afternoon on two beautiful horses. The men wore broad hats, large gold watches and heavy fobs while displaying plenty of money. They conveyed to Colonel Vought that they were making a preliminary survey for the railroad and seemed to be quite interested in the road west and north of Madelia."[5]

"Following the robbery, two weeks later, Colonel Thomas L. Vought, began putting two and two together. He recalled the two men who had stopped by his hotel a couple of weeks earlier, purporting to be cattle buyers. He remembered they had certainly asked more than their share of questions about the lay of the land."[6]

When the news of the Northfield raid came to Colonel Vought, he and two friends strategically hightailed it north and west of Madelia to a growth of trees near a bridge at Armstrong Lake. It was the area that the "cattle

Early photo of downtown Madelia, Minnesota. *Courtesy of the Watonwan County Historical Society.*

buyers" had asked about on their way through the town earlier. Vought and his two companions surmised that the robbers might come out of the trees and pass over this bridge. The threesome hid in the underbrush for two nights. Guns loaded and ready, they awaited the possible appearance of the fugitives.

While hiding in the thicket, the three men noticed a young man who was herding cattle nearby watching them. The boy approached the three men and inquired what they were doing there. It was Asle Oscar Sorbel, who lived in the area. That evening, Asle sat and visited with the three men at the bridge.

> *Always the inquisitive boy, Asle, refused to leave until they told him why there were hiding and for whom they were waiting. When he was told they were waiting for the Northfield bank robbers, the lad's curiosity was satisfied. He now knew what was happening and had a pretty distinct idea of the tactics of the outlaws and what to expect. As he left the three men, he commented, "Gee! I'd love to take a shot at those fellows with dad's old gun."*[7]

It was milking time at the Sorbel farm, just after sunrise, on Thursday morning, September 21, 1876. Ole, Asle's father, thought to himself as he rolled out of bed, "I've got the milking and the chores to do. Asle will help I'm sure." The cattle, in no hurry, ambled along munching snatches of grass in the road on the north side of Lake Linden. Ole tied up one of the milk cows near the road in front of the family home, sat down on a milking stool and began to milk.

Ole looked up and saw two strangers walking by on the road. One had a mustache and the other whiskers—Jim Younger and Charlie Pitts. And as the men passed by Ole, they gently stroked the cow's back and offered Ole a friendly, "Good morning." Ole responded in a friendly manner as he continued to milk the cow. Meanwhile, Asle Oscar was coming up from the barn with a milk pail and saw the brief interaction. "I stood in the gate out of ear shot until they moved on," Asle said years later. "Then I say to my father, 'Them's the two robbers.' Father said, 'I did not think so, as they looked like nice men.' I went out on the road and their toe prints showed in the mud they having worn out their boots. I showed that to father and said, 'Look here. I will show you how nice they are.'"[8]

Embolden by his conversations with Colonel Vought at the bridge the night before, Asle began to see the picture. Robbers around! Adventure and

Cartoon of boy milking cow. *Courtesy of* From Norway to Home.

danger—or not! With nervous excitement, he questioned his next moves, "Should I act? Should I not act?" Then adrenaline surged. Fear chilled Asle's mind. But he must and he would take action. Terror, titillation, courage? Courage, it has been said, is "no more than the management of fear, which must be practiced."

"Well," his father said, "Never mind; tend to your business." Asle recalled what happened next:

> *I milked one cow. Then I set the pail inside the fence and started after them. And sixty rods west of our place, I saw where they had walked into the timber. I walked slow until I knew that I was out of sight of them. Then I went to Anton Owen's house and notified him and also to Mads Owen's farm; and then I went west one mile to Guttterson's Grove where I went on top of the roof to see if they had left the timber, but I could not see the three roads from there, being one from New Ulm, one to Madelia and one to Lockstock. And then I went east again on top of a big hill, and there I could see the three roads, but they had not left the timber.*[9]

Getting more and more excited, Asle's raced onward, his mission evolving minute by minute: "I went again to Anton Owen's house and told Anton Anderson, Jens Nilsson and Armund Brustingen to be sure to get on the big hill and watch the roads."[10]

Guri Redholen Sorbel, circa 1890, or some fourteen years after she offered breakfast to the Youngers. *Courtesy of* From Norway to Home *and the Asle Sorbel Collection.*

While Asle was alerting the neighborhood and following the outlaws' trail, two other members of the gang stopped by the Sorbel farmhouse. Guri Sorbel was busy preparing breakfast when she was interrupted by a knock on the door and a request to buy some food. Who were these strangers? She must have wondered. They said they were hunters and were very hungry. They told her they had baked some bread the day before, but it had soured on them. One of the two men put down some money from a roll of bills.[11]

The men asked for breakfast and were told by Guri the meal wasn't ready, but they were welcome to wait while she cooked it. The two men said they could not wait. Taking some bread and butter, they thanked her and disappeared into the timber.[12] Asle's story continued:

> *When I got back home, they told me there were two more men who had stopped in and bought some bread and butter and better I had to let Anton Owen know that there were four of them. I did not go myself for fear the robbers would spy me out and pick me out, so I sent my sister, Mary, to tell them there were four and to be sure to get on the hill and watch the roads and that I was going to take the east road to Madelia, this being 3 miles further on the east side of the lakes.*[13]

Did parents Ole and Guri know that Asle had sent his twelve-year-old sister on such a dangerous mission? Probably not. Most parents would refuse such risk-taking by their children. Nonetheless, Asle, strong-spirited and driven, acted. He begged his father for a horse he could ride to Madelia, eight miles away. Ole said, "No. This robber business was a dangerous thing." Asle insisted. Finally, Ole relented. A team of horses stood nearby hitched to a farm wagon. Asle removed the harness, the hames and horse collar; loosed the girth and straps from the harness; and then unhitched the tug chain. He jumped on the back of the overly fat nag, dug his heels into the horse's ribs and spurred the reluctant workhorse to a gallop heading to the east.

Asle told it this way: "When I got about two miles from Madelia, my horse fell flat in the mud, and I, too. Well I jumped on again and when I got to Madelia, I was all mud from head to foot. The first man I met did not believe me and asked who knew me? I told him that I knew John Owen, and they went after him, and he said he would stand good for that I spoke the truth."[14]

"Robbers are around—if you want to make money, got to hurry up," Asle shouted, though some thought he was half-crazed. He looked ridiculous riding an old workhorse, plastered in his mud, rumpled farm overalls and jacket. A mess!

Midmorning ride of Asle, the "Paul Revere of Watonwan County," riding fast and furious to Madelia, shouting, "Robbers, robbers!" *Sketch by author.*

Most believed the outlaws were out of Minnesota by this time anyway. Several posses had already disbanded. Reward-eager hunters laid their guns aside and went back to their stores and farms.

However, the citizenry, vigilantes and posses were mistaken. By Sunday morning, September 17, Frank and Jesse James had actually escaped to Rock County in Southwest Minnesota.[15]

From there they spurred their mounts toward Dakota Territory. Arriving near the present-day Springdale Lutheran Church and Good Earth Blood Run State Park, they stopped by Peder and Marit Lommen's farmstead. A supper, a night of rest and then on toward Canton, South Dakota. They stopped overnight at the Ole Rongstad homestead and had a confrontation at the Albert Larson farm, where they stole horses. Crossing the Big Sioux River, they rode to Doon, East Orange, Le Mars and Sioux City, Iowa, and galloped "with hair on fire" until they get home safely to Lee Summit, Missouri.

Meanwhile, dashing on, Asle found Colonel Vought on the porch of the Flanders Hotel.

Excitedly, he told the colonel what he had seen and suspected. They both remembered the night at the bridge. Vought sprang into action. Asle Oscar Sorbel, a seventeen-year-old farm boy in muddy, rumpled overalls shouting, "The outlaws are here, the outlaws are here," had just ridden into history—and would forever be known and celebrated—as the "Paul Revere of Watonwan County."

Asle Oscar's Ride

Listen my children and you shall hear
of the morning ride bereft of fear
On the Twenty First of September Seventy-Six
The Younger Boys in a terrible fix
Young Sorbel rides Dad's nag that year.

—AKF

4

ASLE'S ROLE IN THE SHOOTOUT ON THE WATONWAN

Greater love hath no man than this that a man lay down his life for his friends.
—John 15:13 KJV

"If you want to make money, got to hurry up!" shouted Asle as he dismounted from dad Ole's spent workhorse. Colonel Thomas Lent Vought, sitting idly on his Flanders Hotel veranda, looked up at Asle, dropped his newspaper and leaped to his feet. Earlier, Colonel Vought had suspicions, and he had taken precautionary measures.

Now the several urgent telegrams and numerous seemingly wild rumors were apparently confirmed. Sheriff James Glispin, doing sheriff duties just down the street, heard Asle's holler too. Both men quizzed Asle. "The outlaws northwest of town? Are you sure Asle?" "Yes, yes, you'd better hurry up."

Colonel Vought, a take-charge Civil War veteran, experienced in weaponry and hostile action, wasted no time. Hesitation was not a part of his vocabulary. He grabbed his weapons, flung instructions to his hotel help and headed for the stables to saddle his mount.

"Sheriff James Glispin, quickly closing up his office, also vaulted into action. Glispin, serving his third term as Sheriff of Watonwan County, had the respect as a Civil War Veteran with a reputation for settling trouble without violence."[1]

The two men shouted Asle's call for action to several wide-eyed bystanders. They cajoled other disbelieving yet willing citizens before they hit the road. As Colonel Thomas Lent Vought, Sheriff James Glispin, W.R. Estes, Dr.

Flanders Hotel in downtown Madelia where Asle Sorbel found and alerted Colonel Vought. *Courtesy of the Watonwan County Historical Society.*

Overholt and S.J. Severson galloped out of town, they barked orders for three others to follow. C.A. Pomeroy, G.A. Bradford and Captain W.W. Murphy heard the call to arms and followed quickly.

As the word spread, the entire village of Madelia exploded. Shops shut down. Men armed themselves. Citizens dashed to saddle horses, driving teams and buggies, and some even started out on foot. Asle recounted later, "Men started up, and I lent [my] horse to a man to go after the robbers, and rode back home in a wagon."[2]

The robbers knew the country, and it was evident they were making for John Doolittle's horses about a mile from the Ole and Guri Sorbel farm, presumably to buy or steal getaway mounts. John Doolittle pastured around 250 head of cattle and 100 horses at the time. Cole and Charlie remembered being there on the way to Northfield around June 23. Madelia resident Ruth Yates recalled, "Two men on horseback came to John Doolittle's farm in Riverdale Township, and after looking over his herd of horses, took dinner. Said they were from St. Peter hunting land. That night they staid [*sic*] at the Flanders Hotel in Madelia, registering their names as King and Ward. Remaining here until Sunday afternoon. They departed going East. No one suspecting anything from their appearance."[3]

But the Doolittles remembered and, after hearing about the Northfield raid, judiciously moved their prized horses northwest toward Comfrey, Minnesota, and out of reach.

Glispin's party then met a man on horseback who reported that the robbers were southwest of Madelia about four miles. "When the party came in sight of the robbers, they were at the house of John Skarphol. The pursuers had to cross through a ravine. At the same time the bandits passed over a knoll."[4]

It was about an hour after Asle had sounded the alarm that the sheriff came upon the foursome as they crossed a slough south of Lake Hanska:[5]

> *The Hanska slough which they (the outlaws) waded, was a stream ten feet wide and four feet deep with perpendicular banks. The party in pursuit, found they could not cross with their horses. So Glispin and Estes went east and crossed at Schwingler's about two and a half miles, crossing there. Colonel Vought went up stream about one and a half miles and crossed on the bridge, coming down to the right of the robbers, firing occasionally.*[6]

During this time, Captain William Wallace Murphy and his posse headed for the same site as Glispin. Captain Murphy was a Civil War veteran who served under General Philip Henry Sheridan. He had been wounded by a gunshot to the elbow and saber wounds to the head and arm at Piedmont, Virginia. He was captured and imprisoned for three months in Confederate prisons.[7]

After the war, he married and moved to Madelia, Minnesota, where he farmed and raised livestock. Later he would be elected to the Minnesota state legislature in 1871.

On the way to Hanska Slough, the Murphy posse met Valentine Schaleben and her neighbor, who were driving to Madelia. The women warned Murphy that robbers had tried to steal their horses and had run into the Watonwan River bottom and taken cover in the dense wild plum thicket and vines. Murphy moved his men toward the north branch of the river. With Glispin's posse and Murphy's posse, the two groups formed a triangular area around the Youngers, who were concealed in the underbrush.[8]

After the Youngers had left the Sorbel farm, they regretted exposing themselves.

"We were very imprudent…in going to the house for food," Bob Younger would say later, "but we were so hungry."[9]

They were starved. They were tired. Bob, in pain, dragged along. Cole, Jim and Charlie urged him on. They worried about whether the Sorbels believed their story that they were sportsmen. Bob offered to be left behind, but loyal Cole, Jim and Charlie refused to abandon him.

The outlaws then headed for Andrew Anderson's house and told him they were pursuing dangerous outlaws and needed his horses. The ruse did not work. Anderson ran his horses off in an opposite direction.[10]

Suddenly, the outlaws spied Sheriff Glispin and his men on horseback as they were approaching the marshy outlet to Lake Hanska. The sheriff hollered for the men to halt.

The outlaws ran as the sheriff fired a volley of shots in their direction.

"What do you want?" they called out. Glispin replied, "Put your hands up and surrender!" Fully armed with plenty of lead, why should the fugitives surrender?

Both sides opened fire.

The gang then ran due south toward the brushy thickets of the Watonwan River's north fork. The Madelia pursuers temporarily stalled, desperately searching for a place to cross the water. Finally, they found shallow ground and footing for their horses. They spurred onward, quickly closing the gap from the outlaws. "Reaching the other side, Colonel Vought and Dr. Overholt caught sight of the robbers. Dr. Overholt with so good an aim he hit the stick Cole Younger was walking with."[11] (Earlier, Cole Younger had fashioned a cane to assist walking in order to favor his injured leg.)

Hot lead continued to fly. The outlaws fired a volley back. One bullet grazed Sheriff Glispin's horse. "A horse in the pursuing party, owned by a Norwegian, was wounded and it is thought fatally," according to a report in the *Mankato Review* on Tuesday, September 26, 1876.

> *By this time W. Estes ran out of ammunition and went back to Madelia, informing others where to go, and also sent a telegram to St. James.... Meantime, Glispin was shouting orders for some to go to Doolittle's and stay guard.*
>
> *Sheriff Glispin and others came to the Anderson house, where he posted pickets. August Fedder and William Shannon were by the house. Ole Stone on the bluff, G.W. Green on the east, T.L. Vought and Dr. Overholt to the west.*
>
> *Meanwhile armed citizens were arriving on the north side of the river. Captain Murphy after giving directions concerning the horses, then led forward to the river—the river being twenty feet wide and prairie to the water's edge. Here he posted men at equal distances, each with instructions how to act. Some of the names on the picket line were: George*

P. Johnston, C. Pettis, D. Campbell, Charles Ash, George W. Yates, H.P. Wadsworth, O.C. Cole, Issac Bundy, W.H. Borland, T. Torsen, W. Bundy, G. Christopherson, Robert Shannon, Jack Delling, W.H. Witham, D. Brayton, J.A. Gieriet, J.E. Smith, E.A. Loper, F.D. Joy, E.H. Bill, H. Winter, H. Juveland, Joe Crandall, George Carpenter, and others.[12]

Horses, horses, the desperate outlaws needed horses. Then an opportunity appeared. By happenstance, Horace Thompson, president of the First National Bank of St. Paul, was hunting prairie chickens in the area. The hunting party consisted of his son, four ladies and two children in two rented light spring wagons, each pulled by a pair of fine horses, also rented from Colonel Thomas Lent Vought.

Suddenly, Mrs. Andrew Anderson ran toward the Thompsons, shrieking that the robbers were coming. After Thompson calmed her down by telling her to go to her husband out in a field and tell him, he proceeded to change his light shotgun loads to heavier goose loads and began walking toward the robbers.[13]

Cole and the others were surprised to see the Thompson party. "Hell," he thought, "everybody, even ladies, was after them." But the desperate men recognized the two teams and buggies as a godsend—they must have them.[14]

But thinking Thompson and his son were armed with rifles, the outlaws turned and hid in the tall reeds. Thompson saw that Sheriff Glispin was finally able to cross the river and motioned for him "come over here." Hunkered down near an elbow in the river, the robbers hid. By now more than forty men appeared on the scene ready for action.

Asle Sorbel wanted to be part of the action too. He was eager. He was fearless. He had said, "Gee I'd like to take a shot at them with Dad's own gun," to Colonel Vought. But despite his daring and his desire to be engaged in the shootout, he was consigned simply to hold the horses while others began to load, aim and blast away.

The Younger brothers were no strangers to battle. Thrust into volcanic flames of the Civil War from 1861 to 1865, Bob, Jim and Cole acted and reacted with vengeance and righteous indignation against Northern forces.

When father Henry Washington Younger received three bullets to the back by Kansas Jayhawkers and Red Legs near Independence and mother Bersheba was forced to burn her house down because she was accused of supporting and supplying her sons with food, clothing and lodging, it became payback time. Henry Washington Younger, a lawyer, legislator and judge, was a slaveholder but a staunch Union supporter. He had moved from Kentucky, settling near Lee Summit, Missouri, on a farm of between 600 and 2,500 acres. His murder was a purposeless, senseless act by six Federal soldiers under the command of Union captain Irvin Walley.

Then in the summer of 1863, three of the nine Younger sisters and two cousins were arrested and incarcerated in a three-story brick store in Kansas City. They were accused of spying for the Missouri Bushwackers. In August, the building suddenly collapsed and killed four women inside, including one of the Younger cousins.

Cole Younger claimed the arrests happened because the two cousins had witnessed the murder of his father, Henry.[15]

Quickly, the border area exploded into a hotbed of violence between the Kansas Jayhawks and the western Missouri Bushwackers. Cole joined William C. Quantrill's guerrilla fighters. The fighters had emerged as strident Confederate players who believed in slavery and a state's right to secede.

The Quantrills participated in the political struggle that resulted in violence and destruction on a scale unimaginable. On August 21, 1863, Quantrill led his band of about 450 guerrilla fighters into Lawrence, Kansas. They attacked this pro-Union stronghold, killing between 150 and 200 men. They burned and looted the entire town. History would record this "Lawrence Massacre" as one of the worst battles in the Civil War.

Cole Younger left the Quantrill guerrillas in 1863. He joined the Southern cause, serving as captain under General E. Kirby Smith in Louisiana. He continued to engage in battles between the divided states until 1865.

The war over, Cole and Younger siblings Jim and Bob gradually morphed into outlawry. They joined up with the infamous Frank and Jesse James gang. During the next years, the gang's rampage, attacking in part many northern institutions and former Union causes, would engage in numerous self-initiated skirmishes and targeted battles out of revenge and greed. The Younger brothers would be credited, along with the James brothers' gang, for twelve bank robberies, seven train hold-ups and four stagecoach thefts, all leaving eleven citizens dead.

But for how long would the excitement of outlawry tingle and thrill? Outlaw Henry Starr, who rode and robbed in Oklahoma Indian Territory, expressed the allure: "Life in the open, the rides at night, the spice of danger, the mastery over men, the pride of being able to hold a mob at bay tingles in my views. I love it. It is wild adventure."[16]

But now, outlawry was no longer a tingling adventure as the curtain begins to drop. There would be no applause. After the Northfield, Minnesota gun

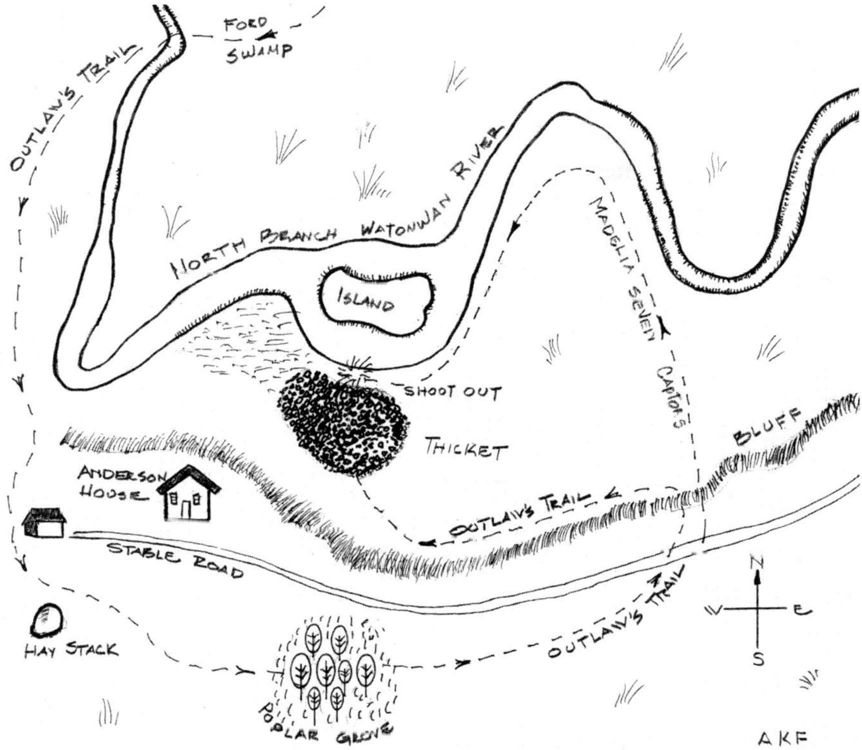

Map of shootout site between Madelia citizenry and the Youngers. *Sketch by author based on archival sketches.*

battle on Division Street and the botched robbery of the First National Bank, they now found themselves in reeds at Hanska Slough. Their final battle breathing hot.

Cole, Jim, Bob and Charlie were surrounded. The firing belched deadly. Black smoke from revolvers, rifles and shotguns puffed and swirled. Deadly lead sought its mark. Whoops and shouts split the air. The hunters were closing in.

"Cole, we are entirely surrounded; there is no hope of escape," Pitts yelled, wounded and wet. "We had better surrender." Cole replied, face blanched and grim, "If you want to go out and surrender, go on. This is where Cole Younger dies."

"All right, Captain," Pitts said, loyal to the end, "I can die just as game as you can. Let's get it done."[17]

Sheriff Glispin called for volunteers to go in and flush the outlaws out. When called to join the perilous attack, sixteen refused. Captain Murphy, as a trained, experienced soldier who was coordinating the final hunt, was shocked by their refusal.

Finally, five men stepped forward. They joined the sheriff and the captain. The seven volunteers were Sheriff James Glispin, Captain William Murphy, George A. Bradford, Benjamin M. Rice, Colonel Thomas L. Vought, Charles A. Pomeroy and S.J. "Slim" Severson. Now assembled, Captain Murphy, a veteran of the Fourteenth Pennsylvania Cavalry, instructed the skirmish line to shoot low as they advanced five feet from one another through the thick willows about five feet high. (A tip: in battle, soldiers were often instructed to aim low because aiming high resulted in many misses.)

The posse knew they had the outlaws surrounded. Captain Murphy, now in charge, addressed the men, "Here's is the way we'll do it, men. Form a line fifteen feet apart and we'll walk right at 'em. When we see 'em, demand their surrender, if they shoot, shoot 'em. Shoot to kill. Keep on shooting till they surrender or all dead, or we are."[18]

As the seven advanced, one outlaw fired his revolver. A fuselage followed on both sides. Charlie Pitts jumped up and aimed at the sheriff. They fired at each other. The sheriff ducked. Missed. Charlie, not so lucky, took a chest hit by Glipsin's single-shot rifle and fell forward, rolled over on his back and died. Rifles, pistols, muskets roared fury. Everyone began shooting. A spray of lead flew everywhere. A slug hit Murphy on the right side of his stomach. Was he mortally wounded? No. Expecting to find blood, he fortunately felt his large briarwood pipe, now splintered, in his vest pocket. Bradford was struck on his wrist by a bullet as he raised his rifle for his first shot. Then Slim Severson yelped, slightly grazed by a projectile.

Now the Youngers took hits from all directions. Charlie was dead. Jim winced in pain, shot in his right thigh. Then his head snapped back as he was hit by Colonel's Vought bullet, which ripped into the left side of his upper jaw and lodged in the roof of his mouth near the back of his throat. (Note: two others in history claimed to have delivered this vicious shot—Yates and Willis Bundy.) Jim dropped to the ground, unconscious, dripping blood profusely. Cole was hit with buckshot; then a bullet hit his right eye and he collapsed, bleeding from the nose and mouth. Bob Younger was shot in the right lung. His injured elbow prevented him from reloading his revolver. (This shot to the lung was later considered to be a factor in Bob's contracting tuberculosis while in prison.)

Bob was the only one standing and conscious. "Surrender. Surrender now!" yelled the captain.

Bob moaned, "Don't shoot anymore…the boys are all riddled."

"Throw up your hands," ordered Sheriff Glispin. Bob held up his left hand. "Throw up the other!" Bob explained that his other arm was broken. Glispin ordered him to move to Captain Murphy and turn over his weapon.

As Bob stepped forward, he came onto higher ground and was suddenly visible to the posse men across the river. One took a shot at Bob, hitting him. It was only a flesh wound but undeserved for one already surrendered. Bob cried out angrily, "Some damned son of a bitch shot me after I surrendered."

Captain Murphy yelled for all men to cease firing. Sheriff Glispin added, "Don't shoot him or I will shoot you!"

Bob approached Murphy and gave up his revolvers. Cole slowly stood, weak from at least eight or nine fresh injuries, and with Jim was marched out of the willows. The shootout at Hanska Slough was over.

The sheriff called for a wagon to be brought forward so that the badly wounded Youngers and the dead Charlie Pitts could be loaded up for a triumphant ride into Madelia. "Colonel Vought walked up to Cole and instantly recognized him as the pleasant Southern gentleman who had lodged at his hotel under the name J.C. King."[19]

After the successful firefight, seven Madelia citizens would be honored and immortalized as the "Magnificent Madelia Seven." The *Martin County Sentinel* reported, "All stood up manfully, not flinching, but each and every one doing his whole duty. In the hottest of the fray, assistance was called for from those in the rear, but not one responded. Then the order to charge was given."[20]

Asle Oscar Sorbel stood by, a close at-hand participant in the fray. He had done his part in the historic capture. Still dressed in his muddy, rumpled overalls, he beamed with a smile of satisfaction as he joined in on the cleanup, helping lift the body of Charlie Pitts onto the wagon, which had just been dragged out of the brush by its feet.

His role was over—at least for now—or was it?

5

A CHEW OF TOBACCO AND "WHY THAT'S THE BOY"

The path less taken is the path of heroes and heroines.
—Terry Mark

The Youngers gave up. Charlie Pitts was stone dead. Sources differ as to who actually shot Jim Younger in the jaw. Mark Gardner recorded it this way:

> *Jim winced in pain as a ball pierced his right thigh. Then his head snapped back as one of Colonel Vought's bullets tore into the left side of his upper jaw and lodged in the roof of his mouth near the back of the throat. He fell to the ground unconscious, blood gushing from his face.... Thirty-three-year-old John M. Robb of Madelia kneeled down and ran his finger between Jim's lips and cleared his mouth, causing the panic in Jim's face to fade away.*[1]

In W.C. Bronaugh's book *The Youngers' Fight For Freedom*, the chapter titled "After Stillwater" describes a second version of Jim's wound in the jaw in a scene after the Youngers' release from prison.

> *The courtly and gallant Yates and Jim Younger sat beside each other at the table. Yates, it will be remembered, was one of the men under command of Captain Murphy who dared to face the fugitives near Madelia. In the final struggle Yates shot Jim and the load of lead tore through the latter's*

cheek and upper jaw, knocking out the teeth and fracturing the bone.... After some hesitation Captain Yates spoke of that scene in 1876. "Do you remember, Jim," said he, "that day after the fight, when I knelt beside you, wiped the blood away from your mouth and endeavored to bandage your mangled face?" "Yes," said Jim, "I remember." then the two shook hands in a brotherly manner, while a tear glistened in the brave captain's eye."[2]

Another account from Cole is slightly different:

Upon Cole Younger's capture, Cole talked openly with George Bradford about a man named Willis Bundy, who had supposedly shot Jim in the mouth. Two posse men, Bowne Yates and his brother George, had been posted on a steep hill overlooking the plum thicket, and when the posse advanced, it was Bowne who had in fact shot Jim. But many persons swore it was posse member Willis Bundy. Willis Bundy was the one who had shot Bob Younger after the bandit had surrendered with a white handkerchief.[3]

Cole Younger was remembered to have said, "If I live to be a free man I will hunt that man down [Willis Bundy] and kill him."

All the various sources graphically describing the action of the shootout and capture agree that the Younger brothers were critically wounded. Jim continued to bleed from his chin. He also had five bullet wounds. His brother Cole, eleven. Bob suffered not only the elbow injury but also a hole in his chest and lung. The three had suffered jointly from exposure and hunger. When Cole took off his boots, his nails fell off. And if their wounds did not kill them, vengeance seekers threatened to hang them on the spot. "It was rumored a trainload of lynchers were on the way, bent on summary vengeance."[4]

The gang's immediate future and ultimate survival teetered near the edge. Would cooler heads prevail? Local newspapers offered accounts of the aftermath.

MAGNIMITY OF THE CAPTORS, when the robbers surrendered, some one from a distance cried out to kill them; but the brave captors having guaranteed protection to the conquered outlaws, indignantly spurned the suggestion, said they pledged their word, and would shoot the first man that dared to fire.[5]

BETTER JUDGMENT prevailed, the men were carefully and tenderly cared for, placed in wagons and brought to town. Captain Murphy observed

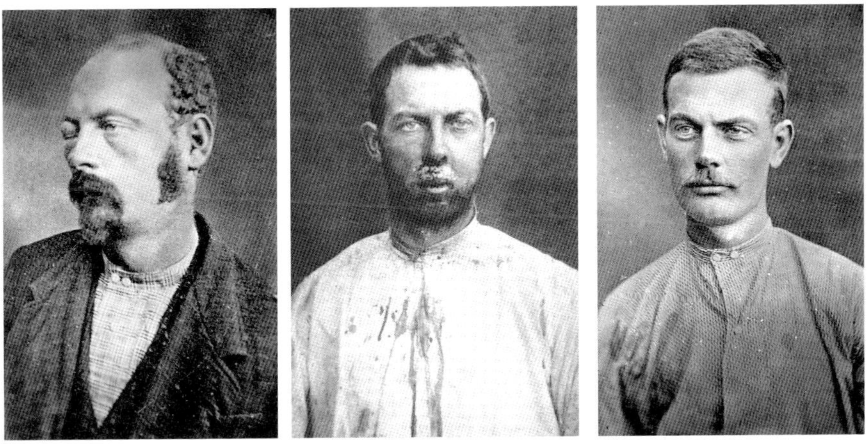

Left: Shot up Cole Younger. *Courtesy of the Northfield Historical Society.*

Middle: Bullet to the mouth of Jim Younger. *Courtesy of the Watonwan County Historical Society.*

Right: Wounded Bob Younger. *Courtesy of the Northfield Historical Society.*

> *their condition and said, "Boys this is horrible, but you see what lawlessness has brought to you* [6]
>
> *The robbers in turn complimented in the strongest terms, the bravery of their captors, and said when forced to surrender, that they much preferred to surrender to such men, instead of the detectives and police, who had so persistently pursued them and whom they hated and despised.*[7]
>
> *They recognized Colonel Vought, of the Flanders House, whose guests they had been several weeks previous, and when taken to the hotel, though badly wounded, Cole Younger pointed out the room he had occupied at the time.*
>
> *They talked freely to their captors and told Captain Murphy they might have killed him, when, before the fight, he had passed within five rods of them posting men, saying that they did not want to shoot him, as it would direct the fire of the pursuers to their hiding place.*[8]
> [Note: 5 rods = 82.5 feet]

Asle related what happened in his own words:

> *Bob Younger held up his left hand and said, "I give up," as the others were all shot to pieces. Bob's right arm had been broken at Northfield, and the*

boys were badly shot up. Cole Younger had one bullet and some buckshot received at Northfield, besides ten fresh buckshot in the body, but he did not pray. He offered to fight two of our best men at once. He said he had been dogged for two weeks in the rain, with nothing to eat but that he could lick two of our best men. Bob slung his left arm around him and said, "Come or we will be hanged." But Cole said he did not care, and that he would just as soon hang today as tomorrow.

Jim Younger was shot in the mouth and five of his teeth had been knocked out, and Charlie Pitts had been killed: I helped lift him in the wagon myself.

Bob Younger asked for a chew of tobacco, and some of the boys swore he should not get any. I went over to Oke Wisty and got a ten-cent plug and handed it to Bob who took about half of it in one chew, and was going to hand it back. But I told him to keep it. Two days after we caught them, they were bound to see me and I had to go up. Bob said "why that's the boy who gave me the tobacco." Cole made quite a speech to me, saying I did my duty, but, that if they had suspected me, they would either have shot me, or taken me along. I also saw them twice at Stillwater afterwards.[9]

Sheriff Glispin's telegram dispatched at 5:30 p.m. read, "Madelia, Sept. 21—Robbers were taken about 8 miles west of here. One killed, the other three wounded, one very badly, probably will not live through the night. Think the two Younger brothers are wounded, and Murphy was wounded in the side, and Geo. Bradford a slight scratch, not serious….J.S. Clarke."[10]

The joy of the capture turned to pity and sympathy. Just as the wounded outlaws were herded into the wagons, women from the Thompson hunting party, especially Mrs. Thompson, offered their kerchiefs and scarves to dress the wounds. Earlier, they had used the same linens to wave and alert the posses to the whereabouts of the gang.

As the wagons with the wounded and one dead robber headed for Madelia, a special trainload of people from other towns appeared about a mile from town. They joined the triumphal procession. Entering Madelia, the wounded robbers and their captors were greeted enthusiastically. In response, the pathetic trio, relieved and amazed, tipped their hats to the crowd.

"A chew of tobacco," a genuine swell of sympathy and prompt medical care surprised the ragged trio. They were stunned. They were gratified. Amazed at how the posse and the people treated them, they would not soon forget. It all started with the offer of a ten-cent chew of tobacco, thanks to Asle Sorbel and Oke Wisty.

On the second floor at the Flanders hotel, Drs. Cooley and Overholt dressed their wounds. Bullets were removed and wounds cauterized. They were given dry clothes and hearty meals. Almost immediately, special trains rolled into Madelia on the Saint Paul & Sioux City Railroad from Minneapolis, St. Paul and Sioux City. For two days, there was a never-ending line of the curious going up to see the men they had heard so much about. "The hired girls were too frightened to stay at the hotel all night so Vought's mother stayed up making biscuits for the multitudes while a Mankato militia group guarded every corner, window and door. Stories circulated that a lynching party from Northfield was on its way."[11]

After the doctor's approval, the captives were allowed to talk to the press and others. Cole maintained that the circumstances of the war as Confederate warriors provided the motivation that brought the Youngers to Minnesota to rob the Northfield bank. He also cited the unmerciful treatment by the Union forces killing his father and forcing his mother to burn her own home for his falling out with the law. Cole's portrayal throughout the rest of his life was, in many cases, a play for sympathy. Cole was articulate, personable and likable. In the events to follow, he used his charm and intelligence consistently and effectively.

Recognizing a rare opportunity, Elias F. Everitt, a photographer from Mankato, raced to take advantage of this historic capture. He staged and photographed the dead Pitts. Pitts's body needed preservation and would soon be placed and packed in ice. Then Everitt placed a chair on the porch of the Flanders hotel and, after gaining permission, brought down each Younger brother for a sitting.

"The crowd was standing room only…as hundreds of people—eight at a time—filed past the robbers.…Bob received several bouquets of flowers from admiring ladies. For the most part of the day though, the scene was one big crying jag. 'The women were melted to sobs and strong men gave way to sympathetic tears,'" reported the *Saint Paul Dispatch*. "Prayers, ardent and fervent, were uttered, and the two brothers [Cole and Jim] clasped each other's hands and gave way to apparent grief, their features quivering in every muscle, and the scalding tears rolling down their cheeks. Many believe in their contrition. Both brothers speak in feeling tones of their dead mother and living sister, and this touches the women wonderfully."[12]

> *Then one lady appeared, weeping along with the rest. She apologized profusely to the brothers and asked for their forgiveness. When she asked if they knew her Bob said, "No, madam I have not had the pleasure." "Don't*

Gallery of participants, *clockwise from top*: Joseph Heywood, Sheriff James Glispin, Bob Younger, Charlie Pitts in death, Jim Younger, Cole Younger and Asle O. Sorbel; *in center*: Bill Chadwell and Clell Miller in death. *Jocoby photograph, courtesy of the Minnesota Historical Society of St. Paul.*

you know me?" she asked again. "Indeed, I cannot recollect you, madam," Bob answered. She then reminded him that she had given him bread and butter. Bob remembered and said, "thank you, we are most grateful."

"O forgive me, sir?" she sobbed, indeed, I did not intend to do it. "I have nothing to forgive you for," Bob gently assured her. "You were very kind to us, and we shall not forget it." "But forgive me sir," she pleaded, "I did not mean to betray you." "Why, really, madam, we never supposed you did. We do not blame you at all. We are only grateful for what you did for us." "But sir, it was because you were at our house you were caught; but it was not my fault, indeed it was not." Finally, to pacify the distraught woman, Bob forgave her, and she immediately brightened. Drying her tears, she said good bye and left the room.

But after the sobbing lady left Bob asked a reporter "who was she?" "Who was the lady," Bob asked. The reporter said that was Mrs. Sorbel, the mother of the lad who alerted the authorities.

"I shall never forget that name," Bob said.[13]

Then Elias Everitt took several historic photographs. One was of the Madelia Seven, and the second was of the young lad Asle Oscar Sorbel, the "Paul Revere of Watonwan County." Another photo of dead Charlie Pitts joined the gallery.

The photo of "the lad in muddy, rumpled overalls," along with multiple newspaper accounts, would cause the undoing of Asle's future life. The photo would be used to promote the notoriety he did not need nor want. That notoriety would force him to always look over his shoulder and to live and endure a life of vigilance and self-imposed secrecy.

The son of Thomas Lent Vought wrote in later years, "But through all the years, there is yet told at Madelia the story of the capture, many different versions, but the outstanding figure the lad of seventeen, be he known by the name of Suborn or Sorbel, it is all the same, his part stand unique in history. He was then as he was all through his life—fearless. Had it not been for him there might have been a different story."[14]

Meanwhile, a delegation from the Twin Cities demanded that the robbers should be turned over to them for trail. Sheriff Ira Barton of Rice county insisted that since the crimes had been committed in his county, the trial would be in Faribault, Minnesota.

On Saturday, September 23 at 6:00 a.m., the robbers and guards left for Mankato, Winona, Owatonna and Faribault under the protection of Sheriff Ira Barton.

Asle headed for home. He and his mother, Guri, had lots to talk about. Ole and Asle's six siblings buzzed and babbled, no doubt, far into the night. Asle would quickly become an unwitting celebrity.

The Madelia Seven would also become celebrities as a group. Their celebrity status, however, would not become as problematic as Asle's. How well did Asle know the Madelia Seven before and after the fiery fuselage?

Asle had gotten to know Colonel Thomas Lent Vought by pure happenstance. The relationship began with the heads-up alert Vought and his companions gave Asle in the area near the bridge Vought was guarding. It was to Colonel Vought at the Flanders House that Asle galloped and delivered the news "that robbers were about."

Vought was born in Wolcott, New York, on April 29, 1833. He served in the Civil War in the Fourteenth Wisconsin Regiment from 1861 to 1865. Then in 1866, he moved to Madelia and began farming, raising stock and opening a stagecoach line. He purchased the Flanders House where on August 23, 1876, two men registered as J.C. King and Jack Ward appeared.

> *They arrived in the middle of the afternoon on two beautiful horses. The men wore broad hats, large gold watches and heavy fobs, and displayed plenty of money. They conveyed to Colonel Vought that they were making a preliminary survey for the railroad and seemed to be quite interested in the road west and north of Madelia.*
>
> *After the robbery two weeks later, Thomas L. Vought began putting two and two together.*[15]

He suspected the two men were the robbers, and when the news reached Madelia he was ready to act.

Later in the shootout "with rapid fire continuing from both sides, two of the posse men were hit in the exchange, although the wounds were not serious. Colonel Vought doubled up from a bullet, which had struck him just above the waist. Clutching his lower vest pocket, Vought was surprised to find the bullet had shattered a large rose-wood pipe he carried. The bullet itself was found in his cartridge belt."[16]

Vought was forty-three years old at the time of the capture.

Asle's father, Ole Sorbel, arrived and settled in Minnesota about the same time Charles A. Pomeroy came with his father to Madelia around 1855. Pomeroy was born in Rutledge, Cattaraugus County, New York. When the call went out, Charles Pomeroy armed himself, mounted his horse and headed after the squad of men who had started out for the scene at the Watonwan. If Asle did not know Charles Pomeroy before the battle, he quickly learned who he was after the shooting. Charles Pomeroy answered Captain Murphy's call to take the robbers out by stepping up and stepping out at the right time. The name Charles Pomeroy, the New Yorker, would be indelibly printed into Madelia's history book as one of the fearless Madelia Seven.

After Asle's shout of alarm, George A. Bradford, a farmer, schoolteacher and clerk of courts in St. James, was one of the first to respond to the call for men to serve on the posse. In a letter to D.E. Hasey, Bradford wrote, "I had raised my gun to shoot, when a bullet struck, or rather grazed my wrist and disturbed my aim, so it was a second or so before I fired. Several shots were fired from both sides and a volley from across the river, from parties there. They could not see us from there, but fired, the bullets cutting the twigs over our heads."[17]

After the robbers were captured and taken to the second floor of Flanders House, George Bradford was assigned to stay with the wounded Bob Younger for the first night.

The Sorbel family may have known or known about Captain William Wallace Murphy. Captain Murphy was born in Ligonier, West Moreland County, Pennsylvania, of Dutch and Scottish heritage. Murphy served in the Civil War under General Philip Henry Sheridan in Virginia. In 1866, Captain Murphy married Inez Atkins and moved to Madelia, where he built a house and began to farm and raise livestock. In the final attack on the Youngers, Murphy organized the "Seven" and took charge. "Murphy was the spirit of the posse of pursuers. Only through his fearless leadership, it is asserted by persons who best know, the surrender of the bank robbers was accomplished….The Youngers too, [later] joined in the eulogy to the captain's bravery."[18]

Murphy was the only one to live out his entire life in Madelia.

The other Norwegian involved in the capture was S.J. "Slim" Severson. Born in Wisconsin, Slim worked as a clerk in a Madelia clothing store and leaped to action when the call came. During the assault into the thicket, he fired on the robbers and then was slightly wounded in the wrist. Though he was simply grazed on the skin, the wound made him acutely aware the gang was serious and would not give up without a fight. Slim moved to Brookings, South Dakota, after his heroism at Hanska Slough and passed away in Milbank, South Dakota, in 1895.

Benjamin A. Rice, six years older than Asle, was "exceptionally expert in the use of arms, being for quickness and accuracy of aim, the equal of any of the robbers he encountered at the Watonwan River."[19] Rice was born in Green County, Alabama, and moved to St. James. He and one other, namely G.S. Thompson, were the two men from St. James who took part in the Younger Brother's capture. Benjamin Rice displayed no reservation, volunteering to fight and capture the robbers.

Sheriff James Glispin responded quickly. The lad Asle Sorbel and his desperate message sounded credible. It was urgent. Glispin, serving his third term as sheriff of Watonwan County, called for help. After the fight, he would not regard himself as a hero but a sheriff just doing his duty as protector and servant of the people of Watonwan County.

However, a Madelia resident and historian in later years had this to say about Glispin: "According to reports from my ancestors and others, Sheriff Gilspin [*sic*] was a young timid soul who would much rather have been elsewhere that day....The sheriff's official capacity forced him to join the posse, shaking badly."[20]

Most records, however, portray Glispin as acting with courage and determination despite possible trepidation, during and through the eventual capture of the Younger brothers. In the battle, he confronted Charlie Pitts in the thickets. As the robbers were scurrying up the bank on the opposite side of the river, dropping to one knee, Glispin fired, hitting Charlie Pitts and

Madelia Magnificent Seven who flushed the gang out of the plum thicket and captured them. *Left to right*: Sheriff James Glipsin, Captain W.W. Murphy, G.A. Bradford, B.M. Rice, Colonel T.L. Vought, C.A. Pomeroy and S.J. Severson. *Courtesy of the Watonwan County Historical Society.*

killing him. Following the Younger capture, Glispin served a fourth term as sheriff of Watonwan County. "He later moved to California, then Spokane, Washington. In his last years he went blind and died in 1890—fourteen years after the Northfield bank raid."[21]

The Madelia Seven, fired by their courage and pure Minnesota grit, would one day be celebrated and honored, by being placed in history's Watonwan County Gallery of Heroes.

But what about the lad in the muddy, rumpled overalls? Was his story ended? Or would a new drama erupt? After all, the Younger brothers had extraordinary memories. As the years passed, would they remember and recall when they had said, "Why, that's the boy who gave me a chew of tobacco." Would they and/or their southern sympathizers remember who turned the brothers in and plan revenge?

6

ASLE VISITS HIS NEMESIS IN STILLWATER PRISON

Now if I had the wings like an angel
over these prison walls I would fly
And I'd fly to the arms of my poor darlin'
and there I'd be willing to die.

—*Vernon Dalhart, "The Prisoner's Song," 1924*

Consider the year 1876. Remarkable. Inventive. Historic. Explosive! Both tragic and lucky events, unequaled, crept and/or blasted their way into the lives of unsuspecting people in unexpected places. Two of those historic Minnesota events began erupting in Northfield on September 7, 1876. They would culminate two weeks later, on September 21, 1876, weaseling into Ole Sorbel's family farm life, uninvited and unimagined. These two events, packed with fire, fury and death, would chisel a permanent mark in Minnesota and American western history.

On a dismal fall day, November 18, 1876, the Younger brothers stood before Judge Samuel Lord in a Faribault courtroom with the following indictments: "The trio is charged with accessory to the murder of Joseph Heywood, accessory to the assault on A.E. Bunker, robbery of the First National bank and Cole as the primary principle and Jim and Bob accessories, to the murder of Nicolas Gustafson."

Each pleaded guilty. Upon hearing the indictment, the brothers were asked if they had anything to say on their behalf, to which Jim and Bob answered, "No." Cole, however, brought the room to tears: "I feel responsible for leading my brothers into the deplorable situation we now find ourselves. I would willingly suffer death in any form—if, by doing so—my brothers could go free." Judge Lord buried his face in his hands and, for several minutes, was incapable of speech."[1]

Judge Lord then addressed the three brothers: "The sentence of the law leaves you life, but robbed of all its pleasures, hope, and ambitions," and sentenced them to life imprisonment in the Minnesota State Prison at Stillwater.[2]

The courtroom went eerily silent. The outlaws' fate was sealed. Then Jim turned to his sister Retta and put his arm around her.[3] The entire courtroom witnessed this spontaneous and warm affection Henrietta displayed for her wayward brothers.

"In announcing the verdict, Judge Lord was so affected that he had trouble speaking. Women began crying; one spirited lady rushed up the aisle saying she wanted to kiss the prisoners."[4]

Leaving the courtroom, the trio was remanded to the Faribault County Jail, where they were locked up for a month.

On November 20, 1876, the three brothers boarded a train in the custody of Sheriff Ara Barton and four guards—John Passon, Thomas Lord, W.H. Dill and Phineas Barton—to be transferred to the Minnesota State Penitentiary at Stillwater. On the way, onlookers threw epithets at them and/or applauded them. Were the Youngers heroes of the South or bloodthirsty desperadoes bent on vengeance? Perhaps both in the minds of the gathered crowd.

> *A Madelia lady, who had helped nurse Cole back to health at the Flanders House, broke through the crowd and told the boys she was grateful they had fallen into her town's "Christian hands." Cole smiled and replied they were sorry too, but probably didn't deserve their kindness. He blamed the Civil War for making him who he was, and added he may have amounted to something had it not been for that dreadful chapter in his life. Bob looked down at her and muttered, "We are rough men, ma'am, and are used to rough ways."*[5]

On November 22, 1876, Cole, Jim and Bob entered the penitentiary as convicts no. 899, no. 999 and no. 901. They walked in subdued, emotions suppressed.

"It did not take the three Youngers long to realize that their new home was 'not fit to keep hogs in, let alone human beings.' The buildings were poorly ventilated, damp and uncomfortable, and overrun with roaches."[6]

The cells were five by seven feet They were each issued a Bible, two cups, one small mirror, a spoon, a face towel, a dish towel, a comb, blankets, sheets, pillowcases, a mattress, a bedstead, springs and a small bar of soap. The prisoners could have visitors—family and friends, once every four weeks.[7] The Youngers were allowed to write two letters a month and draw a ration of tobacco.

When pressured to tell who the outlaws were that got away after Northfield, Cole would never tell. He wrote to his inquisitors, "Be true to your friends if the heavens fall."[8] Cole Younger flatly retorted to a particularly aggressive reporter, "I shall never tell who shot Cashier Joseph Heywood…and the James brothers were not in Northfield and therefore never participated in the robbery attempt."

Cole, however, declared in his memoir that the killer was a drunk Pitts, who shot Heywood through the head.[9] (For more about life in the Stillwater Penitentiary, see John Koblas's detailed research and works *When the Heavens Fell: The Youngers in Prison* from 2002 and *Jesse James Ate Here* from 2001.)

Over the next twenty-five years, the Youngers had a choice—they would either languish or thrive in prison. Which path would they take? Soon after the Youngers arrived at the penitentiary, Warden J.A. Reed immediately put the brothers together making tubs and buckets in the basement. Still the question—languish or thrive? Wither or flourish? Wisely, they made the decision to make every effort to become model prisoners. At this—becoming model prisoners—they were completely successful throughout their imprisonment. Little by little, they earned rewards. Eventually, they were allowed to read in the library. Jim loved to read theology, metaphysics and literature, while Cole preferred historical classics and biographies. Bob read medical books and periodicals.

After serving successfully as postal clerk, Jim advanced to working in the library. Bob became an accounting clerk. Cole distinguished himself as a hospital trustee, caring for the sick in the prison hospital. The hope the Youngers shared during these first years was that after ten years in prison, they would be paroled.

Prison time would be brightened by the tireless efforts by numerous citizens, government officials and several of the wardens to release the Youngers from their life sentence. In time, a cordial relationship grew between the guards and Younger brothers. One prison guard who befriended the Youngers was a young Bernard Francis Casey. Casey would later become ordained as a priest of the order of Capuchin Franciscan Friars. Attributed to a miraculous healing, Father Solanus Casey was beatified by Pope Francis in 2017.

Asle's public photo with pseudonyms as Oscar O. Suborn, Oscar Seeburn. *Courtesy of the Watonwan County Historical Society.*

A surprising visitor who came to visit in 1885 was Warren C. Bronaugh, a former Confederate soldier from Clinton, Missouri. Upon introducing himself to Cole, Warren Bronaugh recalled how he (Warren) had been saved from certain disaster after the Battle of Lone Jack because Cole and his men had warned him that General Blunt of the Union forces was occupying Lone Jack. After this meeting with Cole and the brothers, Bronaugh became the premier advocate for the parole and eventual pardon for the brothers.

Then appeared one of the most unlikely visitors of all—"the kid"—Asle.

"In February 1877, the Youngers had a surprise visitor according to the *Stillwater Gazette*. The brave young chap, Oscar Suborn (Sorbel), who gave prompt notice of the whereabouts of the raiders near Madelia, and was thus instrumental in the capture of the Younger gang, came over Saturday with Solons, and took a look at 'poor Cole Younger painting pails.'"[10]

Eyes staring at each other. Asle and the prisoners. Glaring eyes? Nonchalant glances? Threats? Cordial? Curses? What actually happened? What audacity or naivete would prompt the Paul Revere of Watonwan County, "the boy in muddy, rumpled overalls," to travel to Stillwater from Madelia to take a peek and possibly visit with the brigands?

Emotions were still red hot in Northfield and throughout Minnesota. Some believed the Youngers ought to have been hanged for the murder of highly respected Joseph Heywood.

Others had a soft heart for the Youngers. To people in the South, the Youngers were, if not outright heroes, definitely patriots. They were men who displayed courage in battle and were now victims, corrupted by the circumstances of the war.

Their cells, which were on the ground floor in the second corridor, were often surrounded by a group of visitors. Though the Youngers received no special privileges, many journalists and curiosity seekers wanted to know how they were doing.

In his recollections, *Seventy-Five Years on the Watonwan*, Buster Yates writes,

> *Following their capture the bandits' attitude made a complete switch. They were eloquent in their speech causing young ladies to swoon and admire*

> *them. The adulation followed them all through their years of imprisonment. My father's cousin, Grace Yates, formerly of Madelia, later living in St. Paul, made periodic trips to the prison with goodies, as did numerous other respectable girls.*

Homer Croy reports, "Representatives from women's clubs came to see him [Cole], mostly they wanted to ask if he didn't wish he had led a different life. Cole, always polite, told the ladies sadly that he wished he had. It seemed to give them an immense amount of satisfaction."[11]

Cole Younger would give pious assurances like, "I am proud to say to you we were raised by religious parents and attended Sunday School regular in our boyhood and I had charge of a Bible class, while in Texas at Scyene, Dallas County. I have always respected Christianity. I have known the right and endorse it. I condemn the wrong, but yet the wrong pursued."[12]

After the shootout, a gentle, curious and forgiving south wind began to blow. While the outlaws were being transferred on the streets of Madelia, long lines of local folks watched. Many wept at the sight and expressed sympathy for the outlaws. Some even asked for the outlaws' autographs, and others went so far as to bring gifts.

Guri Sorbel, who had given the outlaws food before the shootout at Linden Lake and whose son Asle had turned them in, pathetically and persistently tried to apologize to the captured trio. Guri wept openly. Bob is said to have remarked "I have nothing to blame you for, madam."[13]

> *While rumors circulated regarding an assault on the prison by friends of the Youngers, stories spread just as quickly that gang members were searching for Asle Oscar Sorbel, the youth who had ridden into Madelia and alerted people to their presence in the Madelia area. While he was directly responsible for their capture, he received little for his efforts. Young Sorbel was paid only a seventy-dollar reward (various records show different figures), and his dash into Madelia had ruined his father's horse. This was small compensation compared to that of the seven men who made the actual capture. Each received $240.00.*[14]

Did Asle Oscar Sorbel consider a second visit to Stillwater? Yes. But soon after his two visits, rumors began to fly. The rumors caused concern—then out right alarm.

Asle knew he had to disappear. "I must go," he announced to his concerned family. Somewhere around 1877 or 1879, he left. Vanished.

After Asle's departure, tragedy struck the Sorbel family. It happened on January 23, 1879. Father Ole went to New Ulm with his wagon and team of horses to do some trading. The distance was around twelve miles.

After finishing his business, Ole left New Ulm at 6:00 p.m. and headed for his Lake Linden area home. When he came to the Shetack road, the team of horses he was driving made a proper turn to the left. As Ole came to the bridge above the Mankato road, one of his horses went just far enough outside the track to miss the bridge. The wagon struck the bridge and overturned. Later, some young men from Cottonwood came along about 11:00 p.m. and found Ole under the wagon with one side of the box lying across his breast. Ole had died. The report said, "The horses would also have perished before morning had they not been discovered, as they were fearfully entangled in their harnesses. Ole Sorbel was buried in the Linden cemetery near the Linden Lutheran church which he and other Norwegian immigrants had founded. It was surmised that Ole had fallen asleep while driving the team of horses home after a long day."[15]

There are several versions of Ole Sorbel's tragic death. Two stories exist regarding the intent of the trip. One tale says he went to sell grain and was returning home with cash.

The other legend says he went to close a land deal, had withdrawn money from the bank, but the "land deal" was purposefully delayed, so he had to travel home with a large amount of money. On the way home he was waylaid, robbed and killed. The team returned home without Ole. Later Ole's body was found in a ravine between Hanska and Madelia. Ole was buried in the Bethel Cemetery."[16]

Whichever story or combination of stories is factual may never be known. Nonetheless, Ole Sorbel, visionary immigrant from Norway, pioneered his way successfully, homesteaded and planted and produced a family, one child of which was a lad who would make the name Sorbel memorable if not immortal.

Years later, at Stillwater Prison, Governor Marshall wrote a pro-Youngers letter. Warren Carter Bronaugh secured a copy and made twenty-five thousand copies. Bronaugh circulated this letter throughout the Midwest and South, as part of his twenty-plus years of stellar and loyal advocacy seeking the release of the Youngers.

Former governor John J. Crittenden of Missouri, to whom Frank James had turned over his revolvers and surrendered in 1882, also endorsed the Youngers' release.

Many newspaper editors in Missouri extolled Cole Younger's virtues as a soldier and gentleman.

However, newly elected governor William R. Merriam of Minnesota vehemently objected to the release of the bloody killer robbers. "No way," declared the citizens of Northfield and several Madelia residents.

Nonetheless, the "Release the Youngers" cry began to grow in scope and intensity. Bronaugh's campaign got a lift when Minnesota governor Henry H. Sibley, elected in 1889, added his influence and voice to the cause. (See W.C. Bronaugh's *The Youngers Fight for Freedom* for an in depth record of the efforts made to release the Youngers from prison.)

Cole, Bronaugh and others argued that Bob needed to be released, as his health was deteriorating. Opponents to the release campaign saw this as a hoax.

Then when Bob grew increasingly ill from consumption"(pulmonary tuberculosis) in September 1889, Retta, the Youngers' sister, came to Bob's bedside in the prison hospital. Jim and Cole, too, were released from their work responsibilities to sit with Bob.

"Bob would ask if they forgave him for his stubbornness in refusing to accept their advice regarding the Minnesota robbery trip. While they reassured him that they did, Bob continued to be guilt ridden and remorseful."[17]

"As Bob's life began to slip from him, he heard a bird calling outside his window. He reminded Cole of the birds back home in Missouri. He asked to be raised so that he might see the sky again and remarked that when he died he thought his soul might rest a moment on the hill outside his cell window."[18]

At the age of thirty-four, after thirteen years in the Minnesota State Penitentiary Bob Younger died. It was 10:30 a.m., September 16, 1889."On September 20, over 800 people packed the Baptist Church in Lee Summit, Missouri, for the funeral of Robert Ewing Younger."[19]

Respect and trust continued to grow for the Younger brothers over the years, even before Bob's death. When the entire prison erupted in flames on January 8, 1884, possibly due to arson, the 350 prisoners were chained together while being moved. Cole offered to help move and relocate the female prisoners. His offer was taken by head guard George F. Dodd under Warden Reed, and he was given a revolver while Jim and Bob were armed with an axe and an iron bar. After the relocation was completed, the Youngers surrendered their weapons.[20]

Finally, the Board of Parole relented, and on July 10, 1901, Jim and Cole were given parole with stipulations. Cole and Jim were ecstatic. They would be free men for the first time in twenty-five years. Among the nine stipulations signed by Warden Wolfer and Governor S.R. Van Sant, the first

Sister Henrietta visiting her brothers in prison. *Courtesy of the Minnesota Historical Society.*

ruled, "He shall not exhibit himself in any dime museum, circus, theater, opera-house or any other place of public amusement or assembly, where a charge is made for admission."

So at ten o'clock on a Sunday morning, July 14, 1901, Coleman Thomas Younger and Jim Hardin Younger were each given a set of civilian clothes and told to "put these clothes on. And you won't have to go back."[21]

The prison door swung open wide. New clothes, new freedoms, new restrictions. Quite a heady pond to swim in after twenty-five years. Would Jim and Cole as new parolees be able to navigate in their coming new world? Would Cole, would Jim, honor the restrictions expected of them? What would happen to Jim? What would happen to Cole? What would happen to Asle?

7
ASLE ON THE RUN

Like a church bell, a coffin, and a vat of chocolate—a supply closet is rarely a comfortable place to hide.

—*Lemony Snicket,* The Blank Book

The news of the capture of the Younger brothers of the Jesse James/Younger brothers gang spread quickly, flooding the country. Telegraph wires buzzed hot. Neighbors in the fields, customers in barbershops and apothecaries talked excitedly.

The news of the shootout and capture would leave an indelible mark in both Minnesota and outlaw history.

When the smoke cleared, guns holstered, seven Madelia citizens stood tall. To the surprise of the hunted and the hunters, the seven stalwart gunfighters in the capture emerged as heroes (see chapter 6).

History dubbed them the "Magnificent Madelia Seven." They would be rewarded, but not much. James Glispin, W.W. Murphy, Thomas L. Vought, George Bradford, Charles Pomeroy, Benjamin Rice and James Severson each received $240.00. Oscar Sorbel, Hans Fryenland and Maddis Lee received $56.25 each.

Thirty-nine others also were given $56.25. Eight received $15.00. Still others who received various amounts of reward money were John Feder Sr., August Feder, George Yates, Bowen Yates, D. Campbell, Charles Ash, H.P. Wadsworth, O.C. Cole, Issac Bundy, W.H. Borland, T. Torsen, William Bundy, G. Christoperson, Robert Shannon, Jack Delling, W.H. Witham,

D. Brayton, J.A. Gieriet, J.E. Smith, Ross Murphy, S.P. Driggers, Doolittle, Jacob Anderson, M.J. Estes, E.A. Loper, F.D. Joy, E.H. Bill, H. Winter, H. Juveland, Joe Crandall, George Carpenter, Thurston Thompson, James McCurdy (rewarded for holding the horses), Noonan, W.R. Estes and Dr. Cooley, who treated the shot-up brothers.[1]

As a reward, Minnesota governor Pillsbury offered Asle Oscar Sorbel a tuition-free education at the university. Asle did not take advantage of the offer.

Asle's $56.25 reward money would later be used to purchase a Black Hills gold ring inscribed with an ornate letter *A* in Old English script on the face.[2] This favorite family heirloom ring is presently in the possession of grandson Dan Sorbel of Rapid City, South Dakota. Dan proudly displays the prize ring, not only to this author but also to the public upon request.

After the fiery outlaw round-up, Asle's notoriety went ballistic. The enterprising photographer Elias F. Everitt scurried from Mankato to Madelia after the capture on the next morning's train. On the train, Everitt jostled for a seat, fending off hordes of curiosity seekers. After arriving in the

Grandson Dan Sorbel of Rapid City displays his grandfather Asle Sorbel's ring. Asle purchased the ring with the reward money he received for the capture of the Younger brothers. *Courtesy of Johnny Sundby Photography, Rapid City, South Dakota.*

hyped little city, Elias was granted permission to take photos of the dead, the wounded, the Madelia Seven heroes and Asle Sorbel.

Elias Everitt posed Asle in his rumpled, muddy overalls, positioning him with his hand on a staged chair. Other local photographers, Ira E. Sumner and William Jocoby, got in on the action as well. It was a bonanza.

Quickly, the entrepreneurial photographers capitalized on the public mood and sold nearly fifty thousand sets of photographs. Asle's photograph was available for sale on trains and in bookstores, and according to the son of Colonel Vought, "Oscar's photo was hawked all over the United States. His picture appeared in the daily and weekly newspapers in the fall of 1876 in *Harper's Weekly* and *Frank Leslie's Illustrated Newspaper*."[3]

T.L. Vought also stated, "Boys of Asle's time, longed to emulate this hero and made up plays in which they would re-enact the prominent part he took in the capture of the Younger Brothers bandit band."[4]

Amid the frenzy, the Younger brothers' memories were acutely intact. The three prisoners remembered.

They remembered the boy in the rumpled, muddy overalls. They remembered Asle's mother, Guri, who sobbed at the sight of the pathetic, bloody, bleeding boys. "Forgive me," she pleaded. Even though Bob said they had nothing to forgive her for. The trio remembered. They remembered the two visits after the capture.

Asle had come, brazenly or naively, to see the brigands at Stillwater Prison. They knew the boy was the rat, the snitch, the tattletale, the Judas, who alerted the authorities. They remembered.

Asle's oldest grandson, David, son of Martin Sorbel, knew his grandfather well, and said, "Sorbel had to drop out of sight for a time because of sympathy for the James Gang."[5]

Oh yes, the Youngers had many friends and sympathizers on the outside. Sympathizers and southern loyalists surged in Missouri and the South. In many cases they were someone or some group who had ridden with Bloody Bill Anderson or William Clark Quantrill during the Civil War as former guerrillas. There were also bleeding hearts and weeping women from the North in Minnesota, whose disgust at vengeance-minded residents kept the controversy aflame.

Current Madelia resident Barb Nelson, staff member at the Watonwan County Museum and curator of "the capture" artifacts, recalled the sentiment to this author, "Asle suspected the possibility of reprisals."

These were dangerous days for Asle. What must he do? Should he lie low? Should he arm himself and stand up and face his adversaries? Should he go into police protective custody? (Of course, there was little or none of that in those days.)

So Asle Oscar Sorbel did what prudence would demand. He vanished. He disappeared! "Forsvinne i fortid." Vamoosed! Gone.

Carleton College professor George Huntington, in his authoritative book *Robber and Hero*, lamented, "Little is known of his life….in connection with the capture…having failed to discover any trace of the brave boy who was the 'Paul Revere' of the final victory."[6]

Descendants of Asle Oscar Sorbel do not know what definitely happened to him. Granddaughter Evelyn Boyer recalled that the horse Asle rode on his historic trip to Madelia was ruined. Because of that loss and the fear of reprisals, Asle was not popular with his family.

Did he change his persona, his name, his location?

It has been speculated by family members—grandchildren Mary Harpestad, Dan Sorbel and Evelyn Boyer—that when Asle dropped out of sight, he changed his name to avoid retribution from gang members. They speculate the names Oscar Oleson or Olesen Suborn were given as an alias for his protection.

In an affidavit dated August 8, 1929, which Asle sent to editor Carl Weicht, Asle admitted to being the person who "caused the arrest and conviction of the Younger Brother. That there was no such person as 'Oscar Olesen Suborn,' but that name was given me in the night of the confusion that then existed and that affiant for reasons then did not wish to make the correction."[7]

So what happened to Asle? He was gone. But where?

The larger question is, what was going on in the times during Asle's disappearance? Between the years 1879 and 1883, Thomas Edison performed a successful test using a carbon filament thread in an incandescent light bulb, which would become the most successful version of this inventive project. The bulb burned for thirteen and a half hours before burning out. Gilbert Sullivan's comic operetta *The Pirates of Penzance* premiered. At Fort Robinson, Cheyenne prisoners led by Dull Knife revolted. Women's rights were signed into law by President Rutherford B. Hayes, giving women attorneys the right to argue cases before the Supreme Court. In 1882, Jesse James was shot and killed by Robert Ford in Jesse's home. President

Asle in exile, joins an unknown troupe. *Sketch by author.*

James Garfield was shot and wounded by Charles Guiteau at a Washington, D.C. train station. Emma Lazaraus wrote her classic poem "The New Colossus." Wyatt Earp and Doc Holliday shot it out against the Tom and Frank McLaury gang in Tombstone, Arizona, in the notorious Gunfight at the OK Corral. During these events, where was Asle Oscar Sorbel?

Asle's years from 1879 to 1883 have been riddled with speculations, confounding family, friends and historians to this day. Great-grandson Stanley Harpstead, in an April 7, 2020 letter to this author, reports, "He [Asle] is listed in the 1880 National Census as being at home with his birth family." Was he actually home, or was the count made in his absence? The mystery grows as historians cling to a couple scanty clues!

Did he join a traveling side show or a circus or a minstrel show?

Asle's daughter Celia, in her autobiography written in verse, includes these words about her father during his disappearance from 1876 (1879) to 1883: "His reward was a sum of money / And lessons in jigging and tap / He danced with a troupe of gay minstrels / And just about covered the map."

Traveling shows were popular in the 1870s and '80s. Freak shows, side shows, minstrel shows, carnivals and circuses traipsed around the country. If Asle joined a minstrel show, where did he go and where did he stay? Wherever Asle landed and/or traveled, he carried in his soul his innate interest, talent and love of jigging, tap dance and music.

Clues from later life, after Asle reappeared, shed light on his three-to-seven-year disappearance. Since he highly prized music and could "cut a rug," he apparently put that love and talent to use.

> *A.O. loved to dance and was very fond of music. He brought home a violin for Alt (Alfred) to learn to play it! The results were not satisfactory, so they traded the violin for a piano. Cora then started piano lessons, paying for the lessons with eggs from Minnie's chicken coop. Ultimately Martin had a slide trombone, Cora a saxophone, and Celia and Cora played the piano. No matter what melody Cora played on the piano, be it "Yankee Doodle," or "Nearer my God to Thee," A.O. would jig or tap dance. Celia said once, "there is an old saying, if you teach a boy to blow a horn, he won't blow up a safe."*[8]

John Phillip Sousa, American composer and conductor, universally known as the March King, led his patriotic band for forty years. Among his more popular pieces are "The Stars and Stripes Forever," "Semper Fidelis," "The Liberty Bell" and "The Washington Post." *Library of Congress.*

Second son Alfred (Alt) played the clarinet. According to family lore, Alt played the soulful instrument in John Philip Sousa's marching band in New York City.

John Philip Sousa, the "March King," thrilled audiences with his rousing marches, romantic waltzes and stirring melodies throughout the United States and world from 1880 to 1932. The brass, both strong and muted, the piccolos in perfect pitch, the trombone double tongued, the clarinet's versatile range entertained audiences with the classics "Stars and Stripes Forever," "The Washington Post," "Semper Fidelis" and an endless catalogue of songs.

"He [Alt] would take the train from Chicago to New York on weekends to play with the great Master."[9] Alt would later turn in his clarinet for a dentist's contra-angled probe tool and practice dentistry in Sisseton, South Dakota.

Asle's son Martin, while attending the University of Wisconsin, studied agriculture but also relished music, playing drums in the university band.

Was it through nature or nurture, or both, that Asle's love and passion for music flourished in his children?

Asle and Tomina's son Dr. A.R. Sorbel practiced as dentist in Sisseton, South Dakota. *Courtesy of* From Norway to Home *and Sorbel collections.*

Did Asle, while in self-imposed exile, join a musical group? After all, he was light on his feet. He radiated a cheerful smile. At his young age, he relished the zest and joy of life—even while the fear of reprisal hovered over his head.

Asle, in his one of two letters written in 1929 to editor Weicht of the *Northfield News*, explained, "Some friend of mine came up and squealed and some outlaw got after me and I had to leave." (This was assumed to be in Montana.)

If Asle was in Montana for a time, perhaps he lived and worked on a ranch.

Did he ride the range? Was he a cowboy? Did he have exposure to livestock and particularly horses? Somewhere, as indicated by his later life and profession, he learned the art and skill of the care and treatment of horses.

Did Asle learn to handle a gun while away? We know he owned a .32-caliber revolver. He used it appropriately. Grandson David Martin Sorbel surmised,

> *During his late teens and early twenties he must have roamed the west. At least he learned how to shoot a gun. Dad* [Martin] *tells of the time that he was asked to hold a horse's head, so Grandpa could put it out of its misery. Grandpa had a big forty-foot barn in town and often brought horses to town to treat them. This time, the horse was beyond treatment, and he told Dad to take the horse to the far end of the barn, turn him around and hold the head steady. Grandpa pulled out a pistol and, without seeming to aim, put the horse out of his misery with a single shot.*[10]

Back at Stillwater, during the years 1879 to 1883, rumors circulated about an assault on the prison by friends of the Youngers. Other threats swirled about. "Friends of the Youngers supposedly hunted Sorbel and allegedly found him on two occasions living in Montana. When the young man (Asle) was asked if he was the one who had ridden into Madelia, Sorbel immediately sensed danger and insisted it had been his brother."[11]

There was no mystery about the whereabouts of Cole Younger and brothers Jim and Bob. As convicts no. 899, 900 and 901, they were tightly secured behind iron bars during the years Asle disappeared—1879 to 1883.

In prison, they worked. At first making tubs and buckets for Warden Reed, after a time Cole and Jim advanced to second-grade prisoners, working in the Seymour and Sabin Thresher factory. Cole made sieves, and Jim made belts. Bob could not straighten his injured arm, so he was given a therapeutic job painting. Finally getting library privileges, the trio was able to read and study. A reporter asked Cole one day if he and his brothers had specific duties in prison. Cole replied:

> *No, Jim and I do very little as we are on the hospital list, but Bob performs various duties. I occupy much of my time in theological studies for which I seem to have a natural inclination. It was the earliest desire of my parents to prepare me for the ministry, but the horrors of war, the murder of my family and the outrages perpetrated upon my poor old mother, sisters and my brothers destroyed our hopes that any of us could be prepared for any duty in life except revenge.*[12]

Cole and Jim, dealing with health issues, spent several months in 1882 in and out of the prison hospital, as well as in their beds in their cells. Word got to the Youngers that on April 3, 1882, Jesse James was shot and killed by Bob Ford in a cowardly assault. Bob Younger was greatly saddened by the murder of his friend Jesse. Jim was less sad, if at all. Jim Younger and Jesse James seldom agreed in their common outlaw life. Cole philosophized about it and continued to deny (keeping his big secret secret) having anything to do with Frank or Jesse James.

In his undisclosed location around 1882, it appeared, Asle was making plans for his next move. Where would he land? What would he do?

The big secret, his role in the capture, would lie buried deep within his soul for the rest of his life. Lips sealed. Eyes and ears alert. Vigilance—until one day...

8

A SUDDEN REAPPEARANCE

From the end, spring new beginnings.
—Pliny the Elder

The Younger brothers, securely lodged in Stillwater Prison, idling their days away, hoping and negotiating for a legal escape, wondered, "Where is that boy, that Madelia snitch?"

Cole had said after the capture that he would have shot Asle or taken him captive.

The Sorbels, too, on the farm near Madelia, wondered—puzzled and praying about the whereabouts of their beloved, vanished son, Asle Oscar.

Then a surprising find surfaced—like a whiskered prospector spying gold flakes in the gravel bottom of French Creek or a bespectacled archivist searching dusty, musty records, jolting upright and blurting, "Eureka!" Plain as day. Among the list of homesteaders' names settled in 1883 in Nutley Township, Day County, South Dakota, is a name tucked quietly in the center: "A.O. Sorbel."

The record reads, "Dates of settlement of homesteaders are as follows, 1883, Lars A. Knude, E. Stavig, Christian Haaseth, *A.O. Sorbel*, G.S. Gunder, and Mikel Moen, Soren and Carl Bendickson, Mike and Frank Schmaus, J. Rassier, M. Rauschwater, A.E. and Martin Erickson, J.A. Vannebo, C.T. Sellevold and Hans Anderson" (emphasis added).

The name Nutley may evoke a smile and surely a question or two. Where was Nutley Township? What was Nutley Township. Why so named? The records report: "Nutley Township is one of several townships located in the northeast corner of Day County. The land is very productive, with most of the farms being diversified, raising small grain and livestock.…The sloughs and potholes in the township provide very good duck hunting."[1]

A survey of the topography reveals, "Nutley Township [w]as a very rolling township with much rough stony land, in fact, it is the roughest township in the county, and no doubt has more rocks to the acre than any other township in the county, however, when the rocks are removed the land is very productive."[2]

Enter our imaginary bespectacled archivist who surfaced still another surprise: "Sorbel Tree Claim." The Sorbel tree claim is located in Section 13 of Nutley Township. "In 1882, Asle and Minnie Sorbel paid the $4.00 required by law for Timber Culture to encourage the growth of timber on the western prairies.…The grove still stands, and the trees are very tall."[3] Author's note: The tree claim proves A.O. Sorbel came to Nutley Township; however, the details of the post are in error unless it was recorded later. Asle and Minnie Westgaard were not married till 1890. Other records show Asle claiming and settling the land in 1883.

Asle Oscar Sorbel reappeared sometime in 1883. He quietly slipped into view, seven years after the 1876 shootout, in this most unlikely place—Nutley Township, Day County, Dakota Territory. (South Dakota would become a state in 1889, three years later.) (Another puzzlement according to Sorbel family researcher great-grandson Stanley Harpstead, is that Asle "is listed in the 1880 National Census as being counted at home with his birth family." So a mystery remains.)

When Asle broke out of his self-imposed exile—wherever he found himself—his journey(s) ended. He had already decided to plant roots, figuratively and literally. Where would he go? What would he do? For reasons unknown, he homesteaded, settled and began to farm land that he heard was available in Day County, South Dakota.

> *At 24 years of age he claimed a homestead of not only the 160 acres allotted but also the tree claim of 160 acres. The maximum allocation of land available was 480 acres which was divided between a homestead, a preemption claim, and a tree claim of the 160 acres. The land was not all that desirable. There were sloughs and hills and no roads.*
>
> *Day County itself is made up of a high terminal moraine with rolling hills and rocky, sandy outcrops. There are very few trees. Tall prairie grasslands cover the area. Around the sloughs and many lakes, some native trees grew, but the overall landscape was somewhat hostile.*

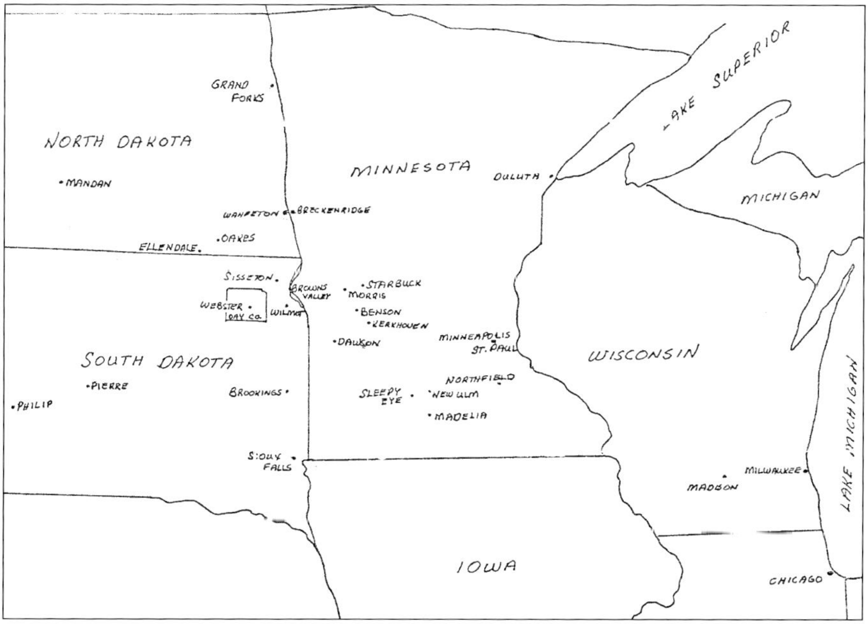

Map of Day County. *Courtesy of* From Norway to Home.

> *Each year brought new settlers to Dakota Territory. In 1883 when Asle settled, only 50 settlers in Nutley and Liberty Townships claimed land and began to farm. When the Westgaards (who would become Asle's inlaws) settled in 1885, there were already 105 families, so the good land was quickly being settled. By 1886, the great Dakota immigration was waning.*[4]

Asle farmed or had a renter farm the stubborn rocky soil with high hopes. Son Reuben Sorbel, then of Rapid City, South Dakota, in a letter dated January 29, 1988, to Oscar Lindholm of Green Mountain Falls, Colorado, said that "his father never farmed but rented the land, so that was some of his income." Few settlers at that time, in that place, realized that a terminal moraine is a glacially formed accumulation of debris that results at the end of a glacier. That debris may consist of irregular soil, rock and trees that have been pushed by glacial activity. This glacial activity, called a geomorphological process, happened thousands of years before.

This author grew up and lived at the final edge of the glacial push called the Coteau Hills, which bordered the vast Jim River Valley. (*Coteau* in French simply means "hillside.")

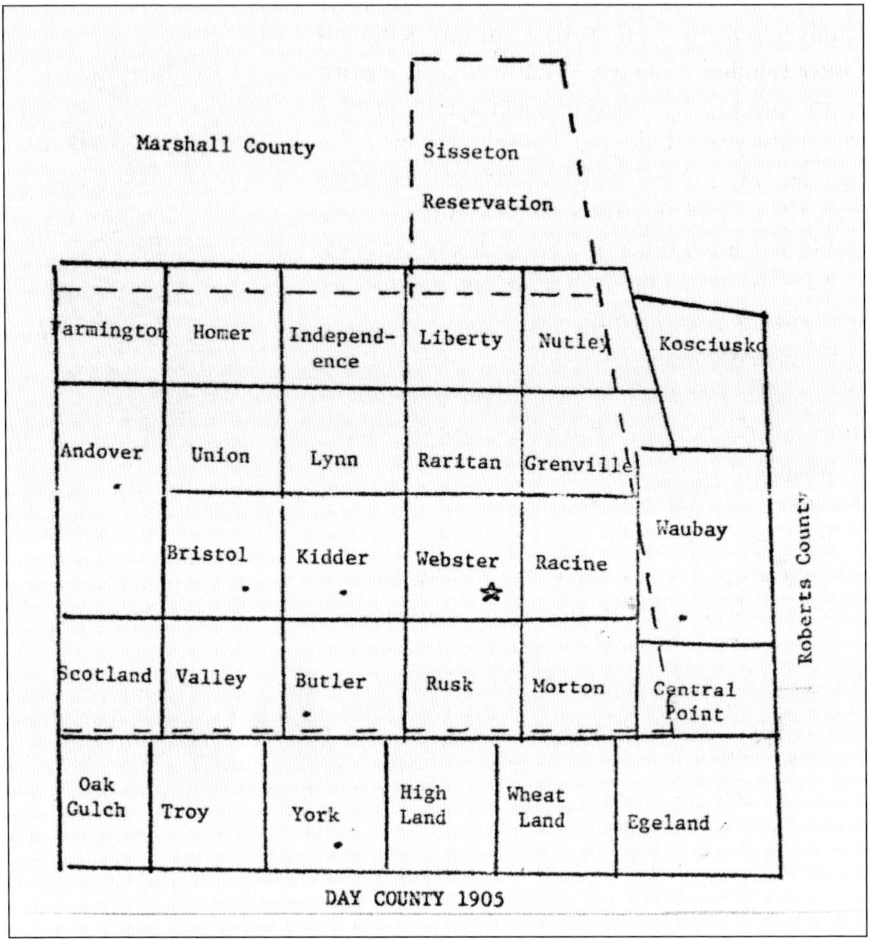

Map of Nutley Township. *Courtesy of* From Norway to Home.

In this environment, Asle planted walnut trees using seeds brought from Minnesota. Since being born and raised where the hardwoods of Minnesota flourished, he refused to be satisfied planting cottonwoods or "wildings" collected along nearby bodies of water as other homesteaders were doing. This stand of walnuts would provide bountiful nuts for munching and baking while also bringing pride and memories to and for his descendants.

Asle also began practicing as a veterinarian. Why and how a veterinarian? Did he learn veterinary skills from where he came from in Montana? Did he go to school? Did he simply pick it up since he was an "independent, enterprising, resourceful, and self-assured young man," according to his family? Son Reuben Sorbel, in his letter to Oscar Lindholm, writes, "I know that he was an apprentice to a Dr. Rissom [spelling unreadable] for many years I do not know." It is possible that he was trained in Montana or soon after arriving in Dakota Territory. Eventually, Asle would become known in the area as Doc A.O. Sorbel, the best "horse doctor" in the region, specializing in treating horses.

Asle's wife, Tomina Westgaard Sorbel, known as "Minnie." *Courtesy of* From Norway to Home *and Harpstead Collections.*

When Asle was thirty-one, he met Tomina Westgaard. Tomina, eighteen, had just moved from the Kirkhoven, Minnesota area to Nutley Township. Cupid's arrows flew, and Asle and Tomina fell in love and were married.

Tomina "Minnie" Westgaard was born on July 10, 1872, in Hamar, Norway, to Ole Thoralsen Negaard and Bertha Simmingsdatter Berg Negaard, who came from near Lake Mjosa, Norway. Ole and Bertha emigrated from Norway around 1885, arriving in New York. Four children came with Ole and Bertha. They were Anna, age sixteen, born on October 25, 1869; Tomina "Minnie" age thirteen, born on July 10, 1872; Beata, age nine, born in July 1876; and Olava "Olive," age four, born on September 23, 1881.

> *The family had a typical crossing of the Atlantic ocean. They left Oslo, Norway, by sailboat. To get on board, they had to be rowed out to where the larger ship was anchored. On board were a large number of cattle and animals. There was very little room for the passengers. Each person was responsible for their own belongings.*
>
> *Tomina spent the days knitting. Bertha was not a well person and the unsanitary conditions concerned her. Bertha had been a laundress in Norway for people who had consumption (T.B.) and had never been strong. She was a dedicated and concerned mother and encouraged the girls to keep their hands occupied with meaningful work. Anna was to become a fine seamstress. Minnie became skilled in knitting. Minnie once said to granddaughter Mary, "Yah, I kanit all the vey across the ocean."*[5]

Tomina's mother, Bertha, was attentive to her faith and committed to baptizing and confirming her children. Since Bertha was pregnant during the voyage across the ocean, she gave birth to Albert Theodore Negaard on February 2, 1886, near Kirkhoven, Minnesota. When Tomina's sister Beata became very ill, it was presumed polio, she became crippled and unable to walk.

Minnie walked seven miles to East Norway Lutheran Church, north of Kirkhoven, Minnesota, to "read for the minister" as confirmation classes were called at that time. The family name was changed during this time from Negaard to Westgaard.

It was a common custom to take the name of the farm in Norway as one's surname. As mentioned, *gaard* means "farm." (A personal example: my surname was changed from Gullickson to Fadness since Fadness was the name of the farm in Norway where my ancestors emigrated from. By 1886, when my grandfather Ole Fadness homesteaded in Oak Gulch township, Day County, the name had been changed.)

Ole, Bertha and family moved to Day County from Kirkhoven to Nutley Township between 1887 and 1888. They traveled by oxen and lived in a sod house.

> *During 1886–1887 the weather was severe. Prairie fires, swept by hot winds, burned the prairie dry. In the winter, heavy snowfall was blown about by the same strong winds. The worst blizzard recorded by the settlers was in 1888. The settlers living in their sod homes heated their dwellings by burning prairie grass, which they twisted. Very little wood existed to be used for heat.*[6]

The church played an important role in the life of many of the immigrants. The church not only provided for the spiritual needs of the new Americans but also became a social gathering place for the community to assemble, become friends and work together. By 1886, Fron Menighed, a Lutheran congregation, had been organized.

Family archivists have uncovered the following history from the records of the Fron Church about the Sorbel/Westgaard families. Under the heading Dobt (baptised) are entries that list the name, date of birth, date of baptism, parents and sponsors.

> *Martin Wilhelm Sorbel was born on September 13, 1891, and baptized on October 17, 1891. Parents listed are A.O. Sorbel og Minnie Sorbel. Sponors are Eng Negaard, Karen Negaard, Anne Skaadin and Peter Ringsberg. This was the seventeenth entry in the record book.*

Alfred Rudolf was born on November 12, 1893, and baptized December 25, 1893. Parents are A.O. Sorbel og Minnie Sorbel. Sponsors were Herman Jensen, Kari Jensen, Anna Westgaard and Arthur Hagen.

Under the heading Konfirmerede (confirmed) are entries that list date, name, age, parent and grade.

October 21, 1894, Andreas T. Westgaard, 14, Ole Westgaard, Husbu, sam or dod God Fosteron

October 20, 1895, Olava Westgaard, 15, Ole Westgaard og Bertha God.

October 29, 1899, Albert Theodore, 13¾ Ole og Berthe megit god.

Fron Aegteviede Jordfaestede (Funeral) Lists name, place of residence, date of death, date of burial, age, place of birth.

1890: Anne O. Westgaard, Day Co., S. D., 28th December, 1889, 8th January, 1890, 26, Osterdalen.

1891: Mrs. Berthe Westgaard, Day Co., 18th May, 21st May, 52, ar Redelen, Norge.

1815: Beata Westgaard, 24th November, 27th November, Webster, Fron.

Church life, important for many early settlers, appeared to be significant to the Westgaard family in Dakota Territory. They regularly attended communion at the Fron Church. The children read for confirmation. But life on the prairie was hard for Bertha.

Bertha Simmingsdatter Berg Westgaard, Tomina's mother, died and was buried on the 21st of May as indicated above. She was 52. She had cared for crippled Beata, young Olive, and young son Albert as well as an adopted or foster son Andreas. (He apparently was a cousin of the Westgaard children.) Bertha had been in her land of hope only six or seven years. She had given birth to an American, had attended to the baptism of that child, had adopted a nephew, confirmed a daughter, had settled twice, first in the Kerkhoven, Minnesota area, and then later in Dakota Territory, and now lay in rest on the wind swept Dakota plain, far from her homeland near Lake Mjosa, Norway.

> *After Bertha's death, Ole (Westgaard) became morose and drank heavily. He neglected the younger children. Beata was crippled from the illness she had had when she was 9 years old, and she was now 15. Andreas, the foster son was 11, Olava was 10 and Albert was 5. The family subsisted and Olive remembers they had no curtains in the front room windows.... The housekeeping was neglected and the children did without....Apparently Minnie helped out as much as possible, as it was she, who arranged for the baptismal certificate to be sent from Minnesota, so Albert could be confirmed.*[7]

Asle and Tomina married on July 11, 1890. They took up housekeeping together in a modest but adequate sod house in their early years of marriage. This was not unusual. Many pioneers lived in sod houses where there was a scarcity of timber or stone building material.

Sod houses or "soddys" were made from bricks or layers of thickly rooted prairie grass. A breaking plow, shaped like a wing, pulled by oxen or mules, plowed up segments of prairie, cutting clean through the soil and turning it over. When wood or stones were scarce, sod houses provided a shelter that was warm in the winter and cool in the summer. The walls were eighteen to twenty-five inches thick. The roof was constructed out of poles and sometimes thatched grasses. The interiors were often lined with canvas or stucco walls. Typically, neighbors would help in the building process. It is probable that neighborly fellow immigrants assisted Doc and Tomina Sorbel.

Life became busy—building, farming, planting trees and making veterinarian calls. When Doc Sorbel would leave to visit a sick animal, Minnie never knew for sure when he would return. On many occasions, he was gone for weeks. It was a lonesome time for her to be alone in the sod house on the wind-swept Dakota prairie.[8]

Minnie gave birth to their first son, Martin William, on September 13, 1891. The birth was not without drama:

> *At the time Minnie was to give birth to Martin, her very first child, A.O. was gone on one of his "calls." Minnie's mother had died four months earlier. Minnie's younger sister, Olive, stopped by the homestead one day. Minnie talked her into staying with her. While Olive was there, Minnie's labor began. Late in the afternoon the delivery was imminent. Minnie was able to coerce Olive into going for help. Olive had no alternative, either she would deliver the baby or she would go to the nearest neighbor to ask*

> *for help. That neighbor lived a mile away. For a 10 year old, it was a frightening decision. She chose to go for help but behind every shadow in the advancing darkness she "saw" wild animals or lurking Indians. Every prairie sound was amplified and resounded in her ears. She ran the mile and returned with help before Martin was delivered. Many times in later life, Olive would recount this experience as the most fearful time of her life as a child on the Dakota prairie.*[9]

Second son Alfred "Alt" Rudolph was born the November 12, 1893, also in the sod home.

> *Life on the prairie was hard for Minnie, with A.O. gone for long periods of time. She was alone without transportation, had two young boys to care for. Among her daily chores was to collect and twist hay to burn for heat, and to carry water for the laundry and drinking. Asle and Minnie lived about four miles from the Hanse post office and also about four miles from the Frank post office. The town of Roslyn would not be established until 1914. The Fron Church had been established in 1886 and the village of Grenville had a general store. Webster, 11 miles away, was a thriving metropolis.*[10]

Meanwhile, at Stillwater Prison, during those years from 1890 to 1897, did the two remaining Youngers give any thought about the kid from Madelia—Asle Sorbel? There is no record about any discussion between the two remaining prisoners. What occupied Cole and Jim's minds became their obsession, their attempts to get out. They had no plans to break out. Just be model prisoners. Prove their worthiness. Pray for a pardon. Get released. Enjoy freedom again.

Warren Carter Bronaugh doggedly maintained his twenty-year-long campaign to get the Youngers released from prison. Loyal sister Retta Younger refused to give up. Like laments from the Psalms a great wail swelled up—letters, petitions, personal visits to legislators, editorials by sympathetic publishers, all cajoling, extolling, pleading, even begging for the release of the Youngers.

Cole wrote to Bronaugh on October 28, 1894, calling him, for his stellar prison release efforts, "God's Nobleman."

Among the reasons given by many who pleaded for a pardon were: penitent spirit, victims of the effects of the Civil War and Cole's exemplary war service and kindness to the enemy.

Horace Greeley Perry, just a child whom Cole had befriended in St. Peter, Minnesota, on his way before the raid in Northfield, now a young editor, wrote,

> *I was going to work this morning and saw the birds so free and happy. My thoughts flew right to a couple of prison cells up at Stillwater, and you may believe me or not, I couldn't hold back the hidden tears. I tell you why I can sympathize with the boys so much. I myself am just like the wild, wild things on the hills, and I can enjoy myself more in the woods alone than anywhere else. To be shut up in a parlor is like caging a wild bird, and I tell you, my friend, when you stop to think seriously of the awful of confinement it is a sad thing.*[11]

However, the wardens and Minnesota governors stubbornly resisted. When Governor Merriam of Minnesota was re-elected, the Youngers' hopes were dashed. Also when Albert Garvin became warden in February 1891, as a trained penologist, he pursued a "fearlessly progressive" agenda. No leniency. No parole. No pardon. Ice-cold resolve.

But then a warm south wind began to blow. Henry Wolfer became warden in June 1892. He "placed Jim Younger in charge of the mail and the library, and Cole was sent to work temporarily in the laundry until the new hospital building was completed. Cole quickly became head nurse in the hospital, a position he held until his release. He later referred to the wardens, deputy wardens, and doctors as his friends."[12]

In 1897, Cole was assigned to help prison physician Dr. A.E. Hedback in his office. According to Dr. Hedbeck, "Cole Younger had a charming personality, was a giant intellectually as well as physically, and had a good command of the English language, frequently using quotations from Shakespeare in conversation. I shall never forget his admonition: 'You can run away from every body else but you can never run away from yourself.'"[13]

According to Cole Younger, "As the years went by the popular feeling against us not only subsided, but our absolute obedience to the minutest detail of the prison discipline won us the consideration, and I might say, the esteem of the prison officials."[14] On October 4, 1893, the prison chaplain Reverend J.H. Albert wrote to Warren Carter Bronaugh, that he was anxious "to see the Youngers out."[15]

In the spring of 1894, A.O. Sorbel decided to move his family to Webster, South Dakota. They had "proved up the claim" and planted trees.[16]

Webster received its name in honor of pioneer settler James Perry Webster, who came to the area in June 1880 from Ohio. The Webster settlement, platted in 1881, became incorporated as a village in 1885. After continuing growth, it blossomed into an incorporated city in 1895.

Doc Sorbel purchased a large lot south of the railroad tracks in Webster. Soon he built a barn and paddock. Minnie, pleased at the move, planted a large garden.

They built a two story home on then northeast corner of their property. The barn was west of the house, and the paddock was in the southwest corner of the block.

Asle and Minnie's home in Webster. *Courtesy of* From Norway to Home *and Harpstead Collections.*

The home consisted of a front parlor, a bedroom and kitchen on the first floor and two bedrooms on the second floor. Several years later, they would add a kitchen to the west, making the former kitchen into a dining room, and adding a bedroom over the kitchen for the young boys. There was a back porch and a front porch. The back porch was a favorite place to clean garden vegetables, to sit and read, to play in the summer or on a rainy day.[17]

On the April 11, 1896, Asle and Minnie's first daughter, Cora Madeline, was born. Third son George Thorwald appeared on September 3, 1898. In 1901, son number four, Reuben Bernard, was born on February 1.

Then the heavens rained down grace at Stillwater. The national news proclaimed it. The Younger boys were granted parole after serving twenty-five years in prison. It was July 10, 1901. At long last—freedom.

The heavy prison doors opened and swung wide when Governor S.R. Van Slant, Chief Justice Charles Start and Attorney General Wallace Douglas finally approved the Younger's parole. "The three men reiterated they were satisfied with the conduct of the brothers over a quarter century, and Cole and Jim had earned their parole if any life prisoner could ever do so."[18]

The *Kansas City Star* reported it this way:

> *Immediately after church services, while Cole Younger, head nurse, was at his accustomed post in the prison hospital, and Jim, librarian and postman, was in the library, each was informed that he was wanted "down front." They supposed that they were to see a visitor in the reception room. But the brothers met a deputy warden who handed each of them a suit of civilian clothes with a telescope grip. "Put these clothes on" said the warden, and he added, "you won't have to go back." The brothers put the clothes on without delay.*[19]

Warden Henry Wolfer, being away, had directed his son, Harry Wolfer, to relay the good news. Harry addressed the Youngers: "Boys," he exclaimed with tears in his eyes and a lump in his throat, "you are paroled. The state board has just approved the parole, the warden will be home soon to tell you all the particulars and arrange for your leaving. Probably you will get away tomorrow. Shake."[20]

Cole was giddy when he heard the good news. It was gospel to him. He blurted out, "Why I feel just like a Methodist….I feel like shaking hands with everybody. I haven't a grudge against anybody in the world, dead or alive."[21]

So how did this news affect Doc A.O. Sorbel? Did he know about the parole? It was public news throughout the country. If and when he knew, what would he do? Did he hear about Cole's jubilant "I haven't a grudge against anybody"? Asle's resolve crystallized into solid rock. He would downplay his past role in the entire escapade by remaining stone cold silent. After all, once released, would Cole and Jim Younger plan vengeance on the kid who turned them in?

Asle now had a family to protect. He had a reputation as the finest horse doctor in the area to preserve. He owned a .32-caliber revolver. Had ammo. Would he need it? His loyal wolfhound was always alert and protective.

One sure thing, Asle would keep the big secret. He laid low. Never, ever, mentioned anything. Mute. Silent. That heroic Paul Revere ride to Madelia, Minnesota, back in 1876 would remain locked away—if need be—forever!

But wait a minute, for how long must and would he keep his mouth shut?

9

DUELING BANJOS—ASLE AND COLE

Parallel societies are exactly that. They exist side by side and rarely meet.
—Andy Ngo

Free at last! The Youngers walked out through the iron doors of Stillwater Penitentiary into freedom on July 10, 1901. Freed by a conditional parole, but not by a pardon, they found the sun and fragrant air invigorating. Bemused, Cole and Jim realized the outside world had changed beyond imagination. They were interested in everything, much like a child at a circus. Hidden charms they had only heard or read about appeared everywhere. Electric-powered streetcars, automobiles, Wild West shows, the beauty of the St. Croix River and the Wisconsin hills.

"Stepping out into the street, Cole wore a dark blue serge suit, a blue and white shirt, a white turn-down collar, a gray silk four-in-hand tie, a black wide-brimmed felt hat and calf shoes. Jim, the shorter of the two, was dressed in a dark gray suit, a pink and white shirt, a polka dot four-in-hand tie and a fedora hat."[1]

Freed with the condition they become employed, Jim and Cole were assigned work on the outside. They peddled tombstones for the Peter N. Peterson Granite Company of St. Paul. They soon realized they did not like that occupation and were not good at it. Jim left the job after two months. He found a job as a clerk in a St. Paul grocery's cigar department. Then he left that position and began working for a Minneapolis cigar store.

Cole thrived as a "people person," kindly, approachable and likable.

Cole in prison. *Wikimedia.*

Jim, on the other hand, grew depressed. After failing at a number of jobs and being denied the right to marry his sweetheart, Alix Muller, Jim's gloom deepened. "On October 14, 1902, Jim gave fifty cents for the socialist cause to street violinist Adolph Grether and said, 'Well goodbye, Adolph. I won't see you again.' Grether assumed Jim had received his pardon and was leaving Minnesota."[2]

The next morning, Jim shot himself in the head with a .35-caliber "bulldog" five-shot revolver and died at age fifty-four. He was living in the Reardon Apartments in St. Paul.

Jim scrawled an affectionate note to Alix, his beloved, "To all that is good and true I love and bid farewell—Jim Younger." Jim Younger died, no doubt, mentally tortured due in part from the effects of twelve bullet wounds in his body that preceded the fatal thirteenth, as well as the refusal in the conditions of his parole to allow him to marry his beloved Alix.

Cole was shocked and saddened by the news of his brother's death. But with new resolve, energized by his parole, he knew he must and would go on.

Cole worked a variety of jobs after the tombstone salesman gig. He served as an assistant manager at the Interstate Institute for Liquor and Morphine Habits and then as a supervisor of workmen at the home of St. Paul police chief John J. O'Conner. In the *Mankato Free Press*, Cole was described as "portly, smooth-faced and quite bald. He is an easy, pleasant talker, and shows intelligence to an unusual degree for a man who has experienced what he has."[3]

Meanwhile, the Sorbel family had moved from Nutley Township to Webster, South Dakota—260 miles west of Stillwater, Minnesota, and 250 miles from St. Paul/Minneapolis—hopefully still a safe distance away from any real or imagined threat because of the prison release of the Youngers.

In the nation, 1901 was a landmark year. President William McKinley was shot and assassinated by anarchist Leon Czolgosz, whereupon Theodore Roosevelt became the twenty-sixth president of the United States. Walt Disney, destined to create Mickey Mouse, Minnie Mouse, Donald Duck and a menagerie of fanciful characters, was born in 1901. Bob Marshall, earth lover and founder of the Wilderness Society, was also born in 1901.

Then the news was trumpeted to the nation and beyond that the "Youngers are freed!"

More quietly, in 1901, on April 14, Asle and Minnie Sorbel, after celebrating the birth of fourth son Reuben Bernard on February 1, had him baptized into the life, death and resurrection of Christ in St. John's Lutheran Church in Webster by Pastor O.O. Hafstat.

During the period from 1876 until 1929, Asle Sorbel would keep the big secret closeted away in his mind. No word about his historic ride to Madelia that September day. He never said a peep to anyone—family, friends, neighbors or clients. Historians wonder, was keeping the secret more necessary now than ever since the Younger brothers were out of prison? Was Asle fearful? Simply cautious? Wisely prudent? Quietly modest? Ever vigilant?

Whatever his feelings, motivations or intentions were, he said, in essence, "I will do what I must do." The doctor dove into his work and practiced the demands of his profession in Day County, all the while providing for his growing family in Webster, South Dakota.

"Webster was a well established community. It had wind mills to provide adequate water, streets had been laid out, trees were planted on the boulevards, there was school, many businesses, a newspaper, postmaster, doctor, drug store, hotel and blacksmith."[4] The city of Webster was the perfect place to sink roots—prosperous, declared county seat in 1886, new courthouse built in 1903 and safe haven for Asle Oscar, Minnie and kids. This ideal community, offering schools, medical care, commerce and plenty of opportunities, enabled the young Sorbel family to thrive.

As a rural and farming area, it required a fierce and demanding dependence on horse power. Before tractors appeared on the scene, draft horses were indispensable. Working draft horses needed professional medical care.

By 1890, Asle Oscar had become known as Doc A.O. Sorbel. He was a voracious reader. Described as enterprising and resourceful, he was a self-taught veterinarian under the apprenticeship of Dr. Rissom. "His services were much sought after by the early immigrants. Oxen and horses were a very prized possession of the immigrants and they almost took better care of their animals than they did of their wives and children."[5]

Citizens of the region trusted Doc Sorbel as the area's preeminent horse care provider. One medical procedure among practicing equine veterinarians was, and still is, filing down a horse's teeth. This preventive procedure every twelve to eighteen months kept their sharp dental points working. A mantra in Sorbel's practice defined his belief, "Healthy teeth makes a healthy body." One veterinarian's clients described the process as follows: "Working on horse's teeth, (most of the farm horses were the cold-blooded draft horses) the Vet (as Doc Sorbel) would usually back the horse into a stall with his rear and backed against the manger. The owner or handler would hold the horse by the halter rope near the halter, the Vet would then place the speculum into the horses' mouth and adjust it to fit the front teeth properly, then he would start to spread the mouth open and locking the speculum as he went along to keep the horse from closing his mouth. When he had spread the mouth open approximately 4 to 6 inches, he then locked the speculum in that place. The Vet would then go to work with the tooth nippers, cutting off any high teeth parts that were sticking up higher than the normal teeth. Then he would use the teeth file or rasp and level off the teeth sharp edges. These speculums were made out of steel and were quite heavy for the size and when on a horse there was quite a bit of heavy along side of his mouth from his lips up to his cheeks, should a horse throw his head and hit you along side of the head with these heavy speculums you learned quickly to try and position yourself so that the chances of being hit that way was lessened to a greet degree."[6]

Grandson David Martin Sorbel from Webster, in his memoir, remembered, "Grandpa Sorbel would drive his team and buggy on his tours around the countryside making his rounds. It seemed his main concern was with the treatment of horses' teeth. A farmer's plow horse couldn't do the work with poor teeth and not being able to eat his oats."[7]

Son Reuben described his dad's profession this way:

> *He had a place in the barn to do the work that had to be done. His transportation was by horse and buggy and I remember he would leave the first of the week and perhaps be gone for a week or ten days. It seems that he had special routes each week, as he was gone much of the time. I do know that he traveled many miles. He would get nearly fifty miles on his trips. The weather was one problem he had especially at winter time. Floating teeth and pulling bad teeth the charge was $3.00 to $4.00. Gelding a stud colt, I think, was $5.00. I know he had special hobbles to put a horse or colt down. There was not any knockout shots as that was unheard of in those days.*
>
> *He was paid by check or cash for work he had done. When working with him it had to be done right. He was proud of his work. Many of the farmers would bring their horses to be worked on to town where he was better equipped to do the work. I think the average age of work horses was between 15–18 years. Glanders was very bad, as there was no cure, so the horse was disposed of and the remains buried.*[8]

Glanders disease, caused by *Burkholderia mallei*, is an infectious disease that afflicts primarily horses, mules and donkeys. It can spread to dogs, cats and even humans. Doc Sorbel's .32 pistol, unfortunately, became a handy, but necessary tool in some situations.

Even though called the "horse doctor," Doc Sorbel also treated cattle and other livestock as he made his rounds. Many cows he treated were inflicted with the ailment called lump or lumpy jaw. Lumpy jaw, or Actinomycosis, refers to large abscesses that grow on the head and neck of an infected animal. The worst ailment, which was fatal with no cure, was anthrax.

One veterinarian client of A.O.'s was Oscar Olson from Roslyn, South Dakota. His wife, Edith Olson, remembered, "Oscar Olson always called A.O. for sick animals. One time A.O. and her husband sat up all night with a colicky mare and saved her. Dr. Sorbel was a rather rough old codger but he watched his language around her. He sure knew his stuff as an old Horse Doctor.…Horse doctors or veterinarians back in A.O.'s days worked under very miserable conditions very often.…Back in these days very few of the drugs and preventive medicines on the shelf today were even heard of.… There were no knockout shots. No tetanus."[9]

Edith Olson continued, "Remember when the Vet was about to perform an operation of some type on a horse, one thing he recommended or required was that they take the horse to some nice green grass spot and there throw him down etc. (this was a much cleaner area than up in the dirty dusty areas around the barns and buildings)."

Four months after Jim's death, Cole Younger was granted a "conditional pardon," effective February 4, 1903. Warden Henry Wolfer had written a letter to the Board of Control of State Institutions, which said, "So far as I have been able to find out his [Cole's] conduct has been above reproach in every respect." The pardon, like the conditional parole, was also conditional. Two conditions of the pardon required Cole Younger to not display himself or place himself in exhibition in any way and that he would never return to Minnesota.

Cole happily left Minnesota and headed home to Lee Summit, Missouri, by train. He crossed into Missouri at 3:00 p.m., on Sunday, February 14. He said later, "I was tempted to give out the 'Confederate yell' but I restrained myself."

> *During the first few months after Cole had returned to Lee Summit, Missouri, he was visited by his old friend, Frank James. The old outlaw Frank James, earlier, after a brief time in prison, had been acquitted of all crimes. Frank had begun farming the old Samuel's place only forty miles away from Lee Summit. The two former outlaws discussed a plan to organize a Wild West Show, despite being aware that Cole's pardon forbade any effort to display himself in public.*[10]

Wild West shows were the rage in 1901. When Cole and Jim Younger had walked out of Stillwater into the streets of this other world, they believed their own Wild West days lay behind them. Yet for Cole, thrilled to receive the conditional pardon, a seed had been planted and would soon sprout into a new and exciting venture. The public loved and enjoyed shows like Colonel Cummin's Wild West Show and Indian Congress. Cummins featuring forty-two sanctioned Native American tribes, and Calamity Jane wowed all ages. Not to be upstaged, Pawnee Bill's Historic Wild West Show, starring Annie Oakley, dazzled eager audiences as well. The most popular extravaganza of all was the Buffalo Bill Wild West Show. At the time of the Youngers' release, Buffalo Bill's show would soon leave America in order to play in Europe again from 1902 to 1903. Cole took notice of this entertainment venue and its popularity. He decided he would go into business managing his own Wild West show in partnership with his old pal, former outlaw and colleague Frank James.

Frank and Cole decided to invest in H.E. Allott's Buckskin Bill Wild West Show. They borrowed $67,000 to purchase an interest. The plan called for Cole to serve as manager and H.E. Allott as assistant manager. Frank would be the ringmaster. The name selected would be The Cole Younger and Frank James Wild West Company.

Despite warnings from Warden Henry Wolfer and the Minnesota state auditor, H.C. Dunn, about jeopardizing Cole's pardon, the duo went ahead advertising a show featuring, "Russian Cossacks, American Cowboys, Rough Riders, Indians, Mexicans and broncos."[11]

Cole, when interviewed by the *Minneapolis Journal*, rationalized his business venture by saying, "But I think I am certainly entitled to use my own name either as the owner of the show or as the author of a book."[12]

The book Cole wrote, published and peddled was his autobiography, titled, *The Story of Cole Younger by Himself*, with this subtitle: *Being an Autobiography of the Missouri Guerrilla Captain and Outlaw, His Capture and Prison Life, and the Only Authentic Account of the Northfield Raid Ever Published.* Cole marketed this book at his lectures and shows. The last part of the book originated from the lectures he delivered throughout the Midwest titled, "What My Life Has Taught Me."

The message of the book and later lectures tended to deny his wrongdoing. It lifted Cole up as misunderstood, if not an honorable war hero, protector of truth, justice, women, children and the American way. Critics, however, exposed truths, half truths, exaggerations, anecdotes and even lies. Yet the account was then and is today an engaging and engrossing read.

The Cole Younger and Frank James Wild West extravaganza went on the road on May 4, 1903, filling thirty train cars. The show landed in Galesburg, Illinois, and performed before thrilled audiences. "The show began with a morning parade. Frank James rode in a handsome carriage drawn by a pair of beautiful white horses, with the crowd applauding him. A dilapidated stagecoach filled with town dignitaries followed by a steam calliope. The audience was treated to a free attraction as Lizzie Blondel was shot from a cannon."[13]

> *The packed evening performance was presented inside canvas walls, as the show did not boast a Big Top like most other circuses. Frank headed the Grand Review on one of his favorite horses, followed by the "Congress of All Nations," exhibiting a multitude of colorful flags. Jack Joyce and acrobatic cowboys held the audience spellbound while performing tricks while in the saddle. A detachment of the United States Sixth Cavalry reenacted Teddy Roosevelt's charge up San Juan Hill. Ellis Jordan and a group of daring Cossacks provided thrills aplenty with their galloping steeds and stunts. Cowboys and Indians sparred in theatrical battles. The audience oohed and awed at Mexican bronc busting, an Australian bolo team, boomerang throwers and Shootist C.B. Cantling and his wife, displaying their shooting skills.*[14]

Cole stayed in the background, managing and informally mixing with the audiences. He believed his word was solid that he would not "exhibit himself" according to the stipulations of the conditional pardon. However, the authorities were unhappy with his behavior, as they felt he pushed the boundaries of the conditions of his pardon.

It was obvious that the name Cole Younger brazenly splashed prominently in the name of the Wild West show along with the name of the old outlaw Frank James had public appeal and definite attracting powers.

The show played in Illinois, Kansas, Missouri, Tennessee, Alabama, Washington, D.C., Baltimore, Pennsylvania and York. The reviews were

Promotion poster for Wild West show in Johnson City, Tennessee. *From the* Comet, *June 4, 1903.*

mixed. The show was plagued with troubles. Troubles grew—short-change grafters, traveling gamblers, thieves, poor attendance in some cities, inexperienced horsemen falling off their mounts and newspaper critics challenging Cole and Frank. The *Knoxville Sentinel* wrote, "The Frank James and Cole Younger Wild West Show…proved to have more gamblers and swindlers with it than have been in Cleveland in many a day."[15]

Lawsuits and counter lawsuits swirled. Finally, Cole and Frank had had enough. The show rolled over, gasped and died, terminating in December 1903. The Cole Younger and Frank James Wild West Show had ended up producing both a glorious and ignoble run for seven months. It blasted off like a rocket but ended in a bankrupted whimper.

Back in Webster, a circus of a different flavor entertained the Sorbels. The year was 1904. Asle and Minnie's second daughter, Celia Lawrenca, was born on March 27 (1904–1981). She was baptized on May 29, 1904, into the life, death and resurrection of Christ at St. John's Lutheran Church in Webster by Pastor O.O. Hafstat. "Minnie's children were born at home, assisted by a Mrs. Egeland."[16]

Eventually, all Sorbel babies would be born in the newly built Peabody Memorial Hospital. The new Peabody Memorial Hospital in Webster opened in 1905. The state-of-the-art hospital flourished under its founder, Dr. H.A. Peabody, and his sons, Dr. Percy D. Peabody and Horace Peabody Jr. Many descendants of Asle and Minnie would also be born and receive medical care at the Peabody clinic and hospital until it burned down.

One notable person born at Peabody Memorial Hospital would be newscaster Tom Brokaw, of contemporary NBC fame, in 1940.

John Lawrence Sorbel was born on May 2, 1906. He was baptized into the life, death and resurrection of Christ in St. John's Lutheran Church by Pastor O.O. Hafstat. Oldest son Martin confirmed his baptism at St. John's Lutheran Church on June 3, 1906. Minnie made sure her children studied and memorized Luther's small catechism with the pastor for a period of time.

Asle and Minnie's children. *Reading clockwise*: Martin (eighteen), Alt (sixteen), Cora (thirteen), Celia (five), Reuben (eight), John (three) and George (one). *Courtesy of* From Norway to Home.

With six children, Minnie had "little time for herself. She did all the spinning and knitting. She did some simple sewing of garments. Her sister Anne would make a Christmas dress for Cora each year."[17]

Webster, the county seat, established a fair in the fall. The first fair was held in 1884 and continues to the present day.

> *A.O., a friend to many farmers, offered his paddock for campers for the three day event. Among the campers, would be Indians who pitched their tents, and brought their families, and ponies. The ponies would be entered in the annual horse racing event. Some of the Sorbel children were embarrassed because of this and would arrange to stay at the home of a friend during Fair Time. Minnie eventually saw through this excuse and denied them the privilege of visiting their friends during this event. She (Minnie) was always a gracious hostess and welcomed everyone into her home.*

> *The children would enter canned goods, pickles, and hand work in the Day County Fair competition. Their school teachers would encourage them to be ingenious and to become involved. There is the story that one young Sorbel lad was a jockey for the horse races, riding one of the Indian ponies. I'm not sure it there is any truth to this story, but everyone knows how well the Sorbel children could ride.*[18]

The calls and requests never stopped for veterinarian needs. A typical lament expressed would be, "Come and help us Doc, my horse has laminitis or has colic or has heaves [a disease causing labored breathing]. My heifer needs attention. My livestock is sick. I need your help." Dutifully, Doc would respond, "Coming as soon as I can." Doc A.O. carried his .32 revolver, a "twist" (equine dental tool), a speculum and essential medical instruments, accompanied with his favorite wolfhound on his buggy rounds.

Minnie used her own matched team of horses, Nancy and Kate, for her transportation needs.

> *One day A.O. needed to make a trip to the country on a call. His horse was lame so he took the buggy. As was his custom, he drove across the prairie as fast as the horses would go. The horses fell into an abandoned well. There was nothing for A.O. to do, there was no help nearby to lift the horses out, he himself was not hurt, so he was forced to shoot them. He was furious, but Minnie was so angry and sad that it took many days for her to even speak to A.O. again.*[19]

Doc Sorbel had favorite clients whose farmsteads he would stop by and enjoy a meal together. One of those farms was the Andrew Akerson home about four miles west of Webster. According to a discussion with Oscar Akerson in an interview by Babe Gruby of Webster, "Sorbel would often stop in at the Akerson farm and had many good meals with the Andrew Akerson family. Oscar Akerson's sister, Anna, would play the piano and the 'Vet' would jig! He really enjoyed that. He [Sorbel] did all the Akerson's vet work. He had said that, 'other doctors are good, if there was nothing wrong.' Ha."[20]

Cole Younger's and Asle Sorbel's lives and adventures, ran on parallel tracks for nearly forty years yet in two different geographic settings. Would those tracks ever cross again after what happened in Madelia, Minnesota, in 1876? Would they come to a juncture? If a meeting occurred—would it be friendly or hostile?

10
THE DANCE CONTINUES

We are all bumbling along, side by side, week in, week out, our paths are similar in some ways and different in others, all apparently running parallel. But parallel lines never meet.
—Mary Lawson

Two parallel narratives danced together toward closure in the late 1800s and early 1900s. Asle Oscar Sorbel and Coleman Thomas Younger, once happenstance combatants, now lived far different lives. They shadowed each other at a distance. They lived, not in a common location, but they shared a common timeline. Would they ever collide again like what happened at Hanska Slough and the Flanders Hotel? Would they ever meet and commiserate about the Stillwater Prison detainment and Asle's two visits? Both Asle and Cole had secrets to keep.

By choice or by some inner compulsion, they were champion secret keepers.

Asle could never forget. Asle could never tell. Cole would never tell. Yet would he finally tell? Was Cole, at last, letting the past be the past? Was Cole growing soft, or maturing, or even forgiving?

Was Asle still afraid? Was Asle simply vigilant? Or modest?

After the Wild West show debacle, in 1905 Cole Younger and Frank James went their own separate ways. Frank James stayed in show business. One performance in which he acted was Walter Van Dyke's play *Across the Desert.* Another venue found Frank James again playing a small part in the play *The Fatal Scar* in Chillicothe, Missouri. Cole Younger made a surprise appearance and attended the performance. After the performance, the old outlaw Frank gave a speech on stage and pointed to Cole sitting in the auditorium. Frank gushed, "There is a man who has all the goodness of an angel in his heart. If our Savior was to come on earth and say to me, 'Where can I get a brave and fearless man to assist St. Peter to guard the portals of heaven?' I would say, 'Cole Younger, And I know he would stick to his post all eternity.'"[1]

Even as Frank and Cole grew older, Cole never told or ever confessed to his dying day (almost) his big secret that Jesse and Frank James had anything to do with the Northfield raid.

After authoring his autobiography, *The Story of Cole Younger by Himself*, Cole was instrumental in engineering an electric railroad—the Kansas City, Lee's Summit and Eastern Railroad, in August 1905. After that business venture, apparently Cole still had carnival blood in his veins. For a brief time, he traveled with the Lew Nichols Carnival Company. Then it was time to move on.

Cole enjoyed being loved in Missouri. He endured being despised in Minnesota—mostly.

> *In 1906, Cole caused an uproar in Minnesota with the announcement of his scheduled appearance at a Fourth of July picnic near Kansas City, where he was to give a lecture and show a moving picture film depicting a train robbery. There was to be a small admission for the show. Because of this public appearance, Minnesota's Governor John Johnson wanted nothing to do with the old rascal. "It seems to me, Minnesota is well rid of him," said Governor Johnson, "we don't want him back and I am not in favor of trying to get him back. Let him stay away."*[2]

Back in Webster, the oldest son of Asle and Minnie Sorbel, Martin William, confirmed his baptism into the life, death and resurrection of Christ. His confirmation took place at St. John's Lutheran Church in Webster on June 3, 1906.

Later, Martin attended Webster High School and would graduate between 1910 and 1912. "He left Webster to attend the University of Wisconsin at Madison. While Martin was in Madison, he studied Agriculture. He played drums in the band. He attended the University for two years."[3]

> *Minnie made sure the children attended church and Sunday School. She would wake the boys on Sunday by rapping on the floor register. A.O. (Asle Oscar) would be "busy" when it was time to go to church, so Minnie would take them in her buggy.*
>
> *The family sat together near the front of the church. After the service started, A.O. would come and sit in the back pew. Minnie saw to it… that the children "read for confirmation," attended Sunday School and Luther League, and sang in the choir. She herself attended the meetings of the Women's Missionary Fellowship and knit mittens and made blankets for the church supported Beresford homes. She also made coffee for church gatherings, (hers was the best), and donated her famous fattigmand and donuts for church meetings.*[4]

In 1907, A.O.'s father's property in Minnesota was probated, and A.O. went back to Minnesota. Several of the children went with him and saw their grandmother Guri.[5]

In 1909, Cole undertook another lecture tour.[6] For the next seven years, Cole began to talk about philosophy and religion. He no longer discussed his outlaw days, even when pressed to talk about his past.

When he hit the lecture circuit, he addressed audiences with "What Life Has Taught Me." He did not romanticize crime. In fact, he denounced it.

Many people came to hear the great outlaw brag about his exploits but were sorely disappointed when it appeared he had turned over a new leaf.

"Cole's manager for the tour, which took him through the Midwest, South, and Southwest, was L.A. Von Erickson. Rolland Marquette, the husband of Cole's grandniece, served as the former outlaw's assistant. Cole's objective was that his talk 'might have impressed a valuable lesson on those who took it to heart.'"[7]

Cole was well read. He often and dramatically quoted and paraphrased Shakespeare, poets and the Bible. He liked to include in his favorite speeches a rewrite of John Milton's lines:

> *Tis better to sit with a fool in Paradise*
> *Than some of those wise ones in prison.*

In Webster, it was school, church, community life and work that occupied the Sorbel household. Asle's and Minnie's family had fun too. The family played the fiddle, the piano, the slide trombone, the coronet and the saxophone. Granddaughter Mary Harpestead said, "Much later, while visiting my cousin Dave, on the farm, I learned Minnie could jig also. Dave played a tune on the fiddle and my Dad grabbed Grandma around the waist, and they jigged for several minutes. At 75 years of age she was still very light on her feet."[8]

Then it happened! The two trajectories nudged closer. Cole Younger traveled—of all places—to Asle Sorbel's territory.

He ambled into South Dakota, carrying his satchel, sans revolver, bullets or vengeance, but tucked in his dark suit pocket was his famous lecture, "What Life Has Taught Me." The aging outlaw, no doubt unaware that Asle Sorbel even lived in South Dakota, arrived in the southwest part of the state in Hot Springs. Hot Springs, South Dakota, is famous for its natural warm springs, its growing artist community and the surrounding rugged canyons and pine-covered hills. Hot Springs, called Minnekahta (warm waters) by the original white settlers in 1879, acquired its current name in 1886. Earlier, the Lakota and the Cheyenne Indian tribes fought for control of the natural warm waters. Legends tell of a hostile encounter waged in the hills above the gurgling springs on a peak called Battle Mountain. Fred Evans and others of an entrepreneurial spirit exploited the chemical-free thermal springs and embarked on an ambitious plan to convert the whole town into a health spa. Evans Plunge is a popular tourist attraction to the present day.

Tall, stately and bald, Cole Thomas Younger arrived in Hot Springs to speak at the Morris Grand Theater on July 10, 1911.

He was warmly greeted by his Hot Springs hosts. The local citizens were eager and curious to hear from the key player in the infamous Jesse James outlaw gang. The attendees who packed the theater saw a man who could well be a preacher or a professor. They listened with reverential respect.

He began,

> *Looking back through the dimly lighted corridors of the past, down the long vistas of time, a time when I feared not the face of mortal man, nor battalions of men, when backed by my old comrades in arms, it may seem inconsistent to say that I appear before you with a timidity born of cowardice, but perhaps you will understand better than I can tell you that twenty-five years in a prison cell fetters a man's intellect as well as his body.*[9]

Exterior of the Morris Grand Theater. *Reprinted from archival sources by permission from* Fall River County Herald Star.

Interior of the Morris Grand Theater recently opened prior to Cole Younger's lecture. *Courtesy of the Hot Springs Public Library, David Driscoll.*

Left: Cole at Hot Springs. *Courtesy of the* Fall River County Herald Star.

Right: Two typical productions at the Morris Grand Theater after Cole Younger's July 10 appearance. *Courtesy of the* Fall River County Herald Star, *July 29, 1911.*

The *Hot Springs Star* publicized the event on July 7, 1911, with Cole's photo and a byline that read "Noted Ex-outlaw who will tell the story of his life at the New Opera House, Monday evening, July 10th."[10]

The New Opera House was known as the Morris Grand, "The Classiest Theatre in the Northwest." It featured Chautauqua-like culture and entertainment. After Cole's appearance, one typical future program promoted "Saturday, December 30th Henry Seaton Merriman's play *With Edged Tools* spotlighting an All Star English Company at popular prices. Seats on Sale at Hargen's Drug Store."[11]

Today, the Morris Grand Theater has been transformed into the Morris Grand Gallery. This restored historic sandstone building features an international destination for fine art, jewelry, minerals and gifts. Built in 1911, the Morris Grand Theater was constructed in the Neoclassical style by William Morris to bring plays and other cultural events to Hot Springs. The cornerstone bears the date and the Jewish star, reflecting Mr. Morris's heritage. Morris brought plays from New York and other events to keep the public connected to his East Coast culture.

In the 1920s, it was converted to a silent movie theater until a talking movie theater opened down the street. For a brief period, the Morris

Grand Theater held boxing events, and in the late 1940s, the building became a NRA shooting range. It was used by Dakota Wesleyan Church as the Lakota Chapel.

Cole's introduction continued,

> *Therefore I disclaim any pretension to literary merit, and trust that my sincerity of purpose will compensate for my lack of eloquence; and, too, I am not so sure that I care for that kind of oratory that leaves the points to guess at, but rather the simple language of the soul that needs no interpreter.*
>
> *Let me say ladies and gentlemen, that the farthest thought from my mind is that of posing as a character. I do not desire to stand upon the basis of notoriety which the past record of my life may have earned for me…my soul's desire is to benefit you by recounting some of the important lessons which my life has taught me.*[12]

Gradually, the audience shifted uneasily in their unpadded theater chairs. They began to realize this talk by the great Cole Younger resembled a lecture on behavior and morality rather than a dramatic review of the rough and wild days of outlawry.

And yet, the very presence of this ex-outlaw telling his life story mesmerized that Hot Springs, South Dakota audience.

Cole droned on, "I believe that no living man can speak upon this theme with more familiarity. I have lived the gentleman, the soldier, the outlaw, and convict, living the best twenty-five years of my life in a felon's cell. I have no desire to pose as a martyr, for men who sin must suffer…for the eagle should not be afraid of the storm.…We must learn our lessons in life."[13]

Meanwhile, A.O. Sorbel, as a common man, would be unimpressed by flowery language and philosophical oracles. Whether Doc Sorbel was aware of this lecture or any others, there is no record. Asle was busy. His family was involved. Cora confirmed her baptism on April 2, 1911.

One day Doc Sorbel jumped into his buggy, hollered "giddyap" to his team of horses and headed for Ortley, South Dakota, seventeen miles out of town. He went to the farm of August and Gena Hovland near Ortley. August Hovland, a regular client of Asle's, had need of the gifted horse doctor.[14]

Doc Sorbel, using his twist, examined a horse patient's teeth while attending to other ailments. The Hovlands were always pleased and grateful for the healing Doc Sorbel performed, according to grandson Brad Hovland of Rapid City.

On another day, Doc Sorbel responded to a call to Ivar and Jacobia Larson's farm to treat a horse needing medical are. Ivar Larson is the grandfather of Paul Larson from Custer, South Dakota.

Ivar's son Oscar also became a client of Doc Sorbel, according to Oscar's son Paul Larson.

One horse that Oscar Larson was very proud of was his Percheron stud Ivanhoe.[15] The Percheron is a breed of draft horse that originated in the Huisne River Valley in western France, part of the former Perche province from which the breed takes its name. Percherons are usually gray or black in color. They are powerful animals with high intelligence, great drive and willingness to work.

The Percheron was a favorite of Doc Sorbel's as well. Doc's practice covered a large area. He would typically be gone on rounds for days at a time. Veterinarians, such as Doc Sorbel, assisted in healing a variety of injuries as well as illnesses of the digestive, musculoskeletal, respiratory and endocrine systems. As a specialist in equine care, Doc Sorbel typically treated abscesses, laminitis and various hoof diseases, all requiring expert, experienced and professional attention.

Top: Doc Sorbel's clients August and Gena Hovland. *Courtesy of Bradley and Kris Hovland, Rapid City, South Dakota.*

Bottom: Doc Sorbel's client's Mr. and Mrs. Ivar Larson. *Courtesy of Paul and Karen Larson of Custer, South Dakota.*

Lawrence and Nora Fadness of rural Butler, South Dakota, were typical clients for veterinarian services for their horses and other livestock.

Oscar Larson's prized Percheron draft horse Ivanhoe. The Percheron breed was Doc Sorbel's favorite equine. *Photograph and information, courtesy of Paul and Karen Larson.*

Oscar Larson demonstrates six horses on boss harrow drag. *Courtesy of Paul and Karen Larson.*

Left: A second-generation Doc Sorbel client, Oscar Larson, son of Ivar, at age nineteen. *Courtesy of Paul and Karen Larson.*

Right: Typical Sorbel client horseman Lawrence Fadness of Butler, South Dakota. *Courtesy of Oriette Faye Fadness Rentschler.*

The Fadness horse barn, built by a previous owner as an equine shelter, was the largest horse barn in Day County at that time. It stretched 112 feet in length. Lawrence, needing room for only a modest team of horses, his May and Babe, and two or three riding ponies, used the horse barn primarily for cattle and sheep. Lawrence was thirty years old when Doc Sorbel died in 1930.

At the Morris Grand Theater in Hot Springs, Cole Younger continued his lecture, saying, "Life is too short to make any other use of it. Besides I owe too much to my fellow men, to my opportunities, to my country, to my God and to myself, to make any other use of the present occasion."[16]

Cole Younger's talks were at times obtuse and sanctimonious, as he portrayed himself in a good light. He lifted up religion in general. He avoided and/or was circuitous about any confession of sin. He justified himself as a "good outlaw" in that he never robbed an individual or honest poor. His philosophy, he expounded, was that the banks robbed the poor, and he had merely robbed the rich.

> *Law is a valiant friend.... When the church is destroyed asylums and prisons flourish.... I want to be a drum major of peace.... Every man has some good in him.... Christ's parable of the wheat and tares shows man is a mix.... There is value in a good friend.... I hate liars and false men.... Ladies are divine creatures of God.... There is no heroism in outlawry.... Now that I am a lecturer, not a minister...let the Lord have his own way with you.... A man who walks with God is in good company.... Don't try to fire blank cartridges at the Author of the universe.... Donn't resort to idleness.* [Selected quotes from What Life Has Taught Me.]

Lecturer Cole Younger ended his presentation in Hot Springs, South Dakota, that hot night by saying, "And now, with your permission, I will close with a bit of verse from Reno, the famous poet—scout. His lines are the embodiment of human nature as it should be, and to me they are sort if a creed. He says

> I never like to see a man a-wrestling with the dumps,
> Cause in the game of life he doesn't always catch the trumps,
> But I can always cotton to a free-and-easy cuss
> As takes his dose and thanks the Lord it wasn't any wuss.
> There ain't no use of swearing and cussing at your luck,
> Cause you can't correct your troubles more than you can drown a duck.
> Remember that when beneath the load your suffering head is bowed
> That God will sprinkle sunshine in the trail of every cloud.
> If you should see a fellow man with trouble's flag unfurled,
> And lookin like he didn't have a friend in all the world,
> Go up and slap him on then back and holler, "How'd you do?"
> And grasp his hand so warm he'll know he has a friend in you,
> And ask him what's a-hurting him, and laugh his cares away,
> And tell him that the darkest hour is just before the day.
> Don't talk in graveyard palaver, but say it right out loud.
> That God will sprinkle sunshine in the trail of every cloud....
> But always keep rememberin, when cares your path enshroud,
> That God has lots of sunshine to spill behind the cloud."

Cole Younger's lectures and autobiography expounded truths, half truths, anecdotes, moralism and even lies when fact checked. His words were smothered with denials and alibis.

Yet Cole's scenarios, though partly truthful and partly fictionalized, tucked into his lectures and book, provide an engaging and insightful presentation when listened to or read. Some have tabbed Cole Younger's traveling lecture as a sermon with three points: crime does not pay, stay away from alcohol and embrace God.

In 1913, back in Webster, Donald Kenneth Sorbel was born on November 21. Mother Minnie was forty-one. "For this delivery she was attended to by Dr. Herman. A.O. sat rocking in the chair in the dining room, Minnie was moaning in the bedroom, and Celia had to dry dishes for the hired girl."[17]

Donald was baptized on February 22. "Donald was a lovely child, loved by everyone. At one time his photograph, taken in a sailor's suit, won first prize in a competition."[18]

Cole often attended plays, concerts, lectures and evangelism services after he got out of prison. In 1913, he befriended an evangelist named Charlie Stewart. Their friendship clicked. Cole revealed to Stewart: "As a young man I had three goals in life: to become a Mason, to marry a good woman and to become a Christian."[19]

> *During that year, 1913, the Rev. Thos. W. Webb, pastor of Lee Summit's Christian Church, conducted a six week's revival in August and September. He invited Evangelist Hamilton to preach, assisted by his soloist, Reverend Charles Stewart. Stewart was a Younger family friend who urged Cole to attend the revival.*
>
> *The attendance grew rapidly with the presence of Cole Younger and by the effective preaching of Hamilton. Soon the old brick church could not hold the growing crowd. A large tent was rented with extra seats placed on the vacant lot adjoining the church.*[20]

> *On August 21, 1913, Cole with his niece Nora Hall, attended the fiftieth anniversary of the Lawrence, Kansas Raid, gathering in that revival tent in Lee Summit. Evangelist Orville Edgar Hamilton invited sinners to step up and cleanse their souls of sin. As the choir sang, "To Rid My Soul of One Dark Blot," (Just as I am without one plea), Cole stood up and kissed Nora on the cheek, and stepped forward, caught up in religious fervor. The former outlaw had come to Christ. A stunned crowd watched him shake hands with Reverend Hamilton, and while many whispered his name, they*

> *gathered around to congratulate him. Cole was but one of one hundred fifty-one people saved that day.*[21]

The former outlaw had reasons to convert on that date, August 21. It was the fiftieth anniversary of William Clark Quantrill's raid in Lawrence, Kansas, where the Bushwacker guerrillas viciously murdered, plundered and burned to the ground many buildings.

Many of the attendees remembered that Cole had joined William Clarke Quantrill's guerrillas during the Civil War, as did his brother Jim and Frank and Jesse James. The Quantrills championed themselves as Confederate Bushwackers, battling the antislavery, pro-union Kansas Jayhawkers.

Lawrence Kansas, a Jayhawker hotbed, had become the target of four hundred heavily armed Bushwackers. "Kill, kill," Quantrill shouted to his men. By 9:00 p.m. on that August 21 day, the guerrillas had massacred between 150 and 200 men, most of them civilians. One hundred homes were torched along with numerous businesses, and the absconded with plunder.[22]

Cole, it is purported, did not participate in the killings; several reports stated he saved a number of lives that day. Some historians say Cole had no remorse for this carnage at Lawrence, Kansas. Others say that the tremendous guilt about that incident plagued him all of his life. Cole loved drama and grand gestures, so when he walked forward as a sixty-nine-year-old rascal and gave his life to Christ, he certainly made a splash by choosing that date for his transformation.

The William Clark Quantrill Society and its descendants continue to celebrate Quantrill's life and legacy to the present day. They are called the Missouri Partisan Rangers. (This author, in researching for photos and communicating by email with one contemporary enthusiast, was warned, "Do not criticize the Quantrills," and then the source added this threat to me, "I am a member of the NRA!")

A few days later, Cole spoke to a reporter,

> *My Grandmother Fristoe used to ask me if I ever prayed before I went into battle. I told her I always did, which was true. I never rode where the bullets were whistling around me without murmuring a prayer. But I did not tell dear old Grandma that ten minutes after I got into a fight I was cussin' loud enough to be heard a mile. She intended me to be a preacher, but I missed it. Now I am a Christian. I've accomplished one of the things I set out to do at any rate, and the greatest of them all.*[23]

In 1913, Cole joined the Christian church in Lee Summit. Some have questioned the veracity of Cole's conversion. History does show that Cole continued to attend worship, give his testimony and sing in the choir until his death three years later.

Frank James and Cole continued to visit each other until February 18, 1915, when Frank, at age seventy-two, died from a heart attack and possible stroke.

In 1916, Cole's health began to decline. He was confined to his room at the home he had purchased for his niece Nora Hall and nephew Harry Younger Hall in Lee Summit, Missouri. The secret that Cole had kept all his life was about Jesse and Frank James actually being a part of the Northfield raid. When Cole felt he was going to die, he said he had some private information he wanted to share with Jesse's son Jesse Edwards James and Jackson County marshal Harry Hoffman. "He swore the two to secrecy, then confided in them his role in the Northfield bank robbery, intimating that it was Frank who had killed the cashier, Joseph Lee Heywood. Jesse Jr., true to his word, kept the secret, but Hoffman later published this 'true account.'"[24]

Cole passed away at 8:45 p.m. on March 21, 1916. He had attained the age of seventy-two, the same as his old comrade and colleague in crime Frank James. An autopsy revealed Cole had fourteen bullets in his body. "On the afternoon of March 24, 1916, a large crowd had assembled at the grave. The graveside services were brief, as the longer service had been held earlier in the church. Cole Younger, often called the last of the great outlaws of the West, was laid to his eternal rest beside his mother."[25]

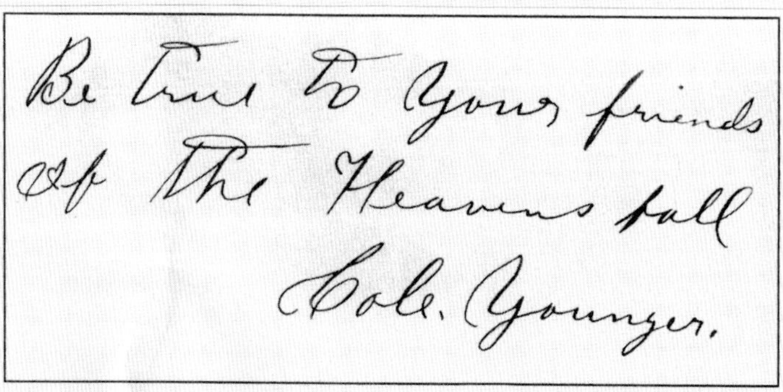

Note scribbled by Cole when asked to identify the other companion outlaws. His refusal, "Be True to your Friends if the Heavens fall." Cole Younger. *Courtesy of the Minnesota Historical Society.*

When Cole was buried, all the unanswered questions about the September 7, 1876 robbery of the First National Bank of Northfield were buried with him. Many secrets and details of the Northfield botched robbery Cole harbored all his life. When interrogated after the capture about whether Frank and Jesse James were involved and who exactly shot Joseph Heywood and Nicolaus Gustafson, that information stayed locked away. Without a word, Cole simply scrawled in bold letters this mysterious answer, "Be True to Your Friends till the Heavens Fall." The pseudonyms J.B. Howard and B.J. Woodson's real identities were never uttered from Cole Younger's lips. Secrets kept. Secrets lost.

However, Asle Oscar Sorbel's big secret stayed locked tightly away—but for how long and why?

11

DENOUEMENT

THE BIG SECRET REVEALED

Secrets, silent stony sit in the dark palaces of both our hearts: secrets weary of their tyranny: tyrants willing to be dethroned.
—*James Joyce,* Ulysses

On October 22, 1916, Donald Kenneth Sorbel, Asle and Minnie's beloved little boy in a sailor suit photo, died.

> *He died after a ten day illness, diagnosed as Intestinal Critis. (Uncle Alt wonders if it wasn't a ruptured appendix). The neighbors had green apples which the children had been eating. Minnie gave Donald enemas for several days to relieve his distress, and he only became worse. Finally someone called the doctor, but there was nothing he could do. After Donald's death, his tiny casket lay beside the dining room door. On the front doorknob of the house someone hung a blue nosegay, as was the custom when a male child dies. The house was filled with the pungent odor of lilies-of-the-valley, a gift to Cora from a male admirer. Grief hung heavy in the home. Donald Kenneth, gently buried in the Webster cemetery, attained two years, ten months, and one day old at the time of his death.*[1]

Cole Thomas Younger's last words were "I have tried to make amends for the crimes of my younger days and hope, under God's mercy, for forgiveness."[2]

Cole's simple headstone bore the inscription: "Cole Younger, 1844–1916, Rest in Peace Our Dear Beloved." The Daughters of the Confederacy later placed a marble plaque next to the headstone: "Cole Younger, Quantrill's Co., C.S.A."[3]

> *Cole loved by some, hated by others, died a much different man than the young outlaw who had wrecked havoc from the Kansas-Missouri Border War of the 1860's to the bungled robbery attempt in Minnesota two decades later. Those in the South—enemies of the Yankee carpetbaggers—had never forgotten his exploits, and to them, he would be remembered as a hero and friend of the common man. Cole did, however, shed some light on some events over the years, if he could and he frequently could not, be believed.*[4]

Progress and changes accelerated in Day County, South Dakota, from 1913 to 1915.

> *The Fairmont and Veblen railroad trackage was laid. The old Frank post office was moved to Eden. George Thorwald Sorbel was confirmed while Alt (Alfred) graduated from high school and left for Northwestern University in Evanston, Illinois to study dentistry. Cora continued to play at St. John's Lutheran Church as the organist....Sports took on a new importance for the family. A.O. and Minnie would attend most basketball games. George was called, "Webster's speedy forward"—but needed to be replaced in games for making too many personal fouls. At a school assembly after a game with Aberdeen, the coach said, "I took a team to Aberdeen last night, but we didn't play them. George Sorbel played them."*
>
> *The girls basketball team was also invincible. Cora was a star on their team. Most games were double-headers, girl's teams and boy's teams, so with a star player on each team, A.O. and Minnie did not miss many games.*[5]

The Sorbels valued education highly. The children were good students. A.O. encouraged them. He prized their academic achievements. He loved their musical passion. Minnie took care of the religious and moral teachings for her family. A.O. would read at any opportunity. Minnie's hands were never still. Minnie knit and crocheted all the time (even in one family photo, she is seen knitting).[6]

Then the events of 1916 exploded. World War I broke out. Europe unleashed its devastating fury. Webster's calm seas were thrust into a new reality—its thin veneer of isolation shattered.

The Sorbels flew the red, white and blue. They were unflinchingly patriotic. In 1917, Martin married Helen Verina Long, and would support the war effort, farming on the farm place north of Roslyn. George was a member of the National Guard in Webster and summoned to duty on the May 2, 1917. George had not yet graduated from Webster High School so his certificate was presented to him in absentia.

Alt would graduate from Northwestern University School of Dentistry and enlist as an officer in the army. Before Alt was sent to France, he married Laura Stavig from Sisseton on May 28, 1918. He met Laura while he practiced dentistry in Sisseton.[7]

George Sorbel received his orders to serve as a cook at Camp Cody, New Mexico. Camp Cody, established in 1916, was named after Buffalo Bill Cody, who died in 1917. Before being renamed, the camp was simply called Camp Deming by virtue of its location near Deming, New Mexico. George would be deployed to France in 1918. The plan for his unit was to first go to the East Coast in order to ship out in midsummer. When his unit got to port, the influenza epidemic was raging so they were kept in quarantine for over six weeks. "This influenza pandemic of 1918–1919, also called Spanish Influenza Pandemic or simply Spanish Flu, was the most severe influenza outbreak in the 20th century. The virus called influenza type A Subtype HINI caused an estimated 25 million deaths world wide."[8]

George's unit finally shipped out and landed in France. George was able to contact his brother Alt, who was already there. One of the letters George received from his mother, Minnie, while he was in service, is dated May 8, 1918:

> *I don't think you better send any money home this month if you should move, you will need it all right….told him to take some money along as he sure need* [sic] *it when he gits over there….Alt couldn't go to Watertown last Sunday. Cora was awfull* [sic] *disappointed. Those Webster people was up to see Cora and they said she looked so good in her uniform. Time goes so fast. It don't seem like its a year seens* [sic] *you got through school, but here it is another year gone by. Wonder how it will be next year by this time and where you boys will be. We thought the war would be over last year by this time but it's still going on….Reub is going on the farm Saturday to take a breaking plow up to Martin…and we will have to take*

> *the cow up so as there ain't anyplace to keep her in town.…I have been thinking I should send some candy but you know I can't make candy. Cora was always the one who made it when she was home.…A.O. is out in the country most of the time now. This is his busy time you know. He uses the car all the time but we still got three horses in town. Reub sure got a pretty horse now and she is pretty frisky and that's what Reub likes.*
>
> *With lots of love from mother.*

Then the thunder ceased. M1903 Springfield rifles, machine guns, grenades and artillery fell silent. The Great War ended. The Armistice was signed on November 11, 1918. Both George and Alt were ordered to stay in France for another six months to help with the clean-up. Before George was discharged on June 28, 1919, he was able to get a leave and spend several days at Nice on the Mediterranean. Alt was also discharged. Back home, sister Cora graduated from nursing school.[9]

Asle and Minnie would enjoy many life changes in the Sorbel household from 1916 to 1928. Reuben Barnard confirmed his baptism on November 19, 1916. Celia confirmed her baptism on April 6, 1919. Martin William Sorbel married Helen Verina Long in September 1917. Alfred Rudolph Sorbel married Laura O. Stavig on May 28, 1918. Cora Madeline Sorbel married Edward Arthur Schwartz on October 5, 1921. John Lawrence Sorbel confirmed his baptism on February 29, 1922. George Thorwald Sorbel, father of Mary Lou Harpestead of *From Norway to Home*, married Evelyn Stavig on July 4, 1924. Celia Lawrenca Sorbel married Manley Hedman on December 30, 1926, and Reuben Bernard Sorbel married Loretta Budde, on October 27, 1928.[10]

Grandson David Sorbel remembered,

> *Grandpa* [A.O.] *would leave town with his team and buggy, however when he was in town, he was always good for a walk down town and an ice cream cone. Sometimes he would get very upset when Grandma* [Minnie] *would put paper under his spittoon when he was sitting in the living room reading the paper. Grandma was a very fastidious house keeper and the thought of tobacco juice on the carpet was more than she could stand. Grandpa would get very insulted and move the spittoon to the other side of the chair.*
>
> *After we moved to the Long farm, the folks joined St. John's in Webster. Richard and I were baptized one Sunday after Church by Rev. F.I. Schmidt in 1925 at the Parsonage. The folks had not gone to church while living*

at Roslyn due to the distance to Webster. After we moved to the area, Dad [Asle's son Martin] *was Sunday School Superintendent for several years at St. Johns. We would often stop at Grandma Sorbel's for Sunday dinner after church. Sometimes Grandpa would be there too. Because of his age, he didn't go out with his team and buggy as often, although he would go out and treat an animal if the farmer would come and get him.*[11]

Eventually, A.O. gave up driving a horse and buggy to and from his rounds around Day County and beyond. He purchased his one and only automobile—a Model T Ford. Sorbel family lore loves to recall and laugh at the many times A.O. would holler "whoa, whoa," when he braked, attempting to stop the skedaddling Model T.

Grandson David recalled a story when his dad (Martin) was going down the road with a team and wagon when the roads were very muddy.

Off in the distance a Model T Ford was doing it's best to keep going in the mud. Dad [Martin] *said Grandpa* [Asle] *was agitated to think a xxxx fool would be trying to drive a car in the mud. As the car came closer, Grandpa suddenly exclaimed, "Why, that's my car!!! Who's driving it?" It was none other than uncle George, who had taken the notion to drive the 20 miles from Webster to see how things were going on the farm. "I,* [David] *never did hear the consequence of that escapade."*

Uncle George seemed to be the chauffeur for Grandpa while he owned that one and only car of his life time. His job came to an end one day when they drove out of the driveway in Webster while Grandpa was in the back seat. The car hit a bump and the old touring top collapsed, coming down and hitting Grandpa on the head. It was said that they kept on going downtown where Grandpa promptly sold the Model T.[12]

He [Asle] *was very broken up the time that Celia and Manley left in 1929 to go to New York. The Sunday that they left, he was out in the yard and I saw tears in his eyes as Celia and Manley drove off in their new 1929 Chevy.*[13]

Then in 1924 the big secret broke free from its decades-old cocoon. Asle Oscar Sorbel would tell. He would tell all. Unencumbered of all or any internal or external restraints, he told the *Argus Leader* what actually happened on September 21, 1876. Later he would write the editor C.L. Weicht of the *Northfield News*, a similar account to the following clarifying story:

Right: Asle Oscar Sorbel in later years. *Courtesy* From Norway to Home.

Below: Asle and boys *left to right*: George, Alt Alfred, Asle, Martin and Reuben. *Courtesy* From Norway to Home.

Asle, as a boy, keeps his lifelong secret. *Courtesy of* From Norway to Home.

I read something in the Argus Leader *about my having been lost sight of and about my name being Oscar O. Suborn. To begin with there never was such a boy with the name Oscar O. Suborn. No one called me that at the time. I supposed they gave me that name to fit, but it never was mine. My name was then and still is A.O. Sorbel and I have lived in Webster for forty one years, having come here in 1883.*

Having been asked to give my experiences in the capture of the Younger boys, I will do so in as few words as possible, and it is a true story at that.

It was September 21, 1876, just two weeks after the Northfield robbery, early in the morning, just after sunrise, my father had got up to milk the cows.

By the way, it had rained for two weeks: it was a kind of drizzling rain falling night and day and it was terribly muddy. We kept the cattle in the road on the north side of Lake Linden. I had gone to the barn with my milk pail, when Jim Younger and Charley Pitts came along. They went each on one side of father and they both stroked the cow's back. They said very cheerfully, "Good morning" to my father. I stood by the gate till they went out of earshot. Then I said to father they were the two robbers. Father said he did not think so, as they looked like "nice" men. I went out in the road, and there two prints showed in the mud, they having worn out their boots. I showed that to father and said: "Look here. I will show you how nice they are." "Well," he said, "never mind: tend to your business."

I milked the cow. Then I set the pail inside the fence and started after them, and sixty rods west of our place, I saw where they had walked into the timber. Then I went to Anton Owen's house, and notified him and also to Mads Owen's farm; and then I went west one mile to Gutterson's Groves where I went on top of the roof to see if they had left the timber, but I could not see the three roads from there, there being one to New Ulm, one to Madelia and the other to Lockstock. Then I went east again, on top of a big hill and there I could see the three roads but they had not left the timber. I went again to Anton Owen's house and told Anton Anderson, Jens Nilsson and Amund Brustingen to be sure to get on the big hill and watch the roads, so the men would not steal a march on us as I was going to ride to Madelia.

> *When I got back home they told me that there were two more men who had stopped there and bought some bread and butter. I had to let Anton Owen know that there were four of them. I did not dare to go myself for fear the robbers would spy me out and pick me…so I sent my sister Mary, to tell them there were four and to be sure to get on the hill and watch the roads and that I was going to Madelia, this being 3 miles further on the east side of the lakes. I went north of our house and kept…the north side of the Timber, so the robbers could not see me across the lake. I rode on a gallop as much as he horse could run and when I got to Madelia, my horse fell in that mud, and I, too. Well, I jumped on again, and when I got to Madelia, I was all mud from head to foot. The first man I met did not believe me and asked John Owen, and they went after him, and he said he would stand good for that I spoke the truth.*[14]

Asle's narrative to the *Northfield News* told all, revealing from his perspective the big secret:

> *Jim Younger was shot in the mouth and five of his teeth had been knocked out and Charlie Pitts had been killed. I helped lift him in the wagon myself. Bob Younger asked for a chew of tobacco and some of the boys swore he should not get any. I went over to Oke Wisty and got a 10 cent plug and handed it to Bob who took about half of it in one chew and was going to hand it back, but I told him to keep it. Two days after we caught them, they were bound to see me and I had to go up. Bob said, "Why that's the boy who gave me the tobacco." Cole made quite a speech to me saying, I did my duty but, that if they had suspected me, they would either have shot me or taken me along. I also saw them twice at Stillwater afterwards. Cole told me he never was so mistaken as any one ever was about father. It was he and Bob that stopped at our house to get provisions. Bob carried then his arm in a sling under his raincoat. They asked father where the best fishing and hunting was, and he pointed it out to them and never by a quiver could they tell that he knew who they were.*
>
> *I was back in the old house two years ago and at Madelia, and they told me they were going to erect a monument in memory of the capture of the Northfield bank robbers, and that my name should go in correctly. The seven men who went into the timber and I got $235.00, the reward offered. But we never received one penny of the $50,000 offered by Missouri and the express companies.*[15]

On August 8, 1929, an affidavit was signed by A.O. Sorbel and also signed and notarized by Andrew Hedman, notary public of the State of South Dakota, County of Day. It reads as follows:

> *A.O. Sorbel of Webster, South Dakota, being first duly sworn on oath doth say, that he is the person that on September 21st, 1876, gave the information to the town of Madelia, Minnesota, that caused the arrest and conviction of the Younger Brothers that robbed the First National Bank of Northfield, Minnesota, on September 7th, 1876. That there was no such person as "Oscar Olesen Suborn" but that this name was given me in the night in the confusion that then existed and that the affiant for reasons then did not wish to make the correction.* [signed] *A.O. Sorbel. Subscribed and sworn to before me this 8th day of August, 1929. Andrew Hedman, Notary Public. My commission expires 8-10-30.*[16]

Asle's second letter, which was dated August 19, 1929, and addressed to editor C.L. Weicht of the *Northfield News*, basically repeated the details of the first letter and added:

> *Dear Sir, I was on a trip, consequently this delay. I am a veterinarian so I go on trips often. Timely, I will send you a picture I took this spring when I was 70 which you may keep. My wife also sent you a picture taken 53 years ago which will ask you to send back as it is the only one I* [have] *left. I will write briefly the raid but as I am a poor writer so will have to put the flavor on it.... This is a true story of the catching of the Northfield Robbers, I also got the picture of the 8 robbers and banker Haywood* [Heywood] *but I suppose you got them if you haven't I can lend it to you. A.O. Sorbel. If you print this send me the paper.*[17]

Asle Oscar Sorbel died on July 11, 1930, the fortieth anniversary of his wedding. Grandson David recalled the shock and grief:

> *One of the Sundays after Church, we stopped to celebrate Grandma's 58th birthday, July 10, 1930. We had cake and ice-cream and spent most of the afternoon in town. Late in the afternoon, Henry Peterson from south of Webster came in and wanted "Doc" to come out to the farm to help with a sick cow. Grandpa, of course, went with him, even though he had not been feeling good for the past few days. It was said that he was seen downtown with his overcoat on, in hot July weather.*

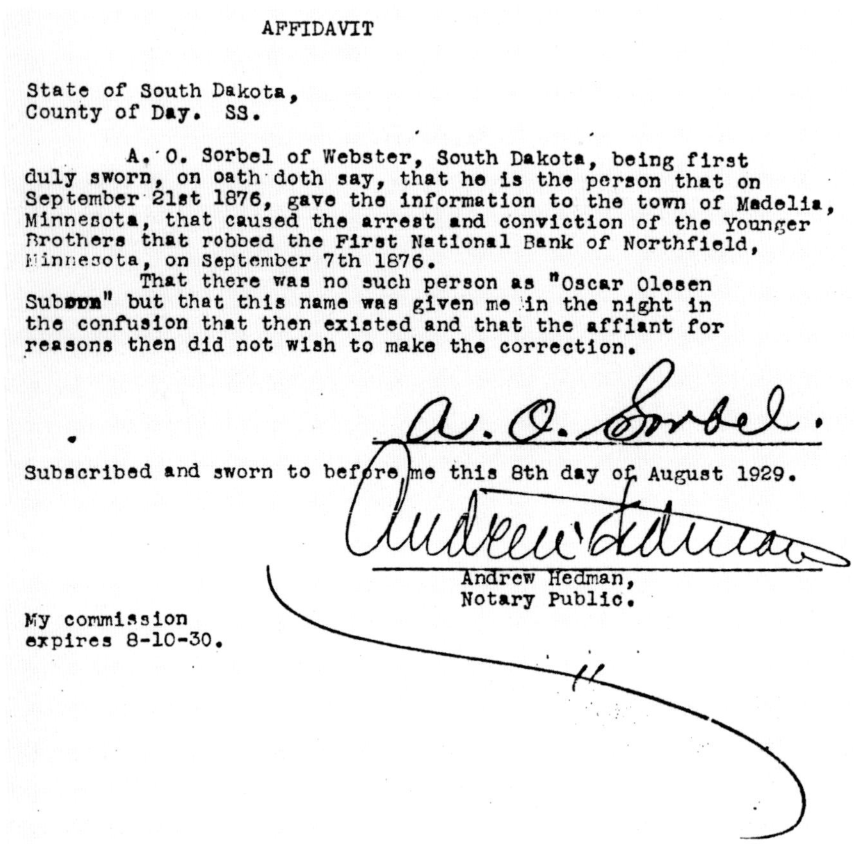

AFFIDAVIT

State of South Dakota,
County of Day. SS.

A. O. Sorbel of Webster, South Dakota, being first duly sworn, on oath doth say, that he is the person that on September 21st 1876, gave the information to the town of Madelia, Minnesota, that caused the arrest and conviction of the Younger Brothers that robbed the First National Bank of Northfield, Minnesota, on September 7th 1876.

That there was no such person as "Oscar Olesen Suborn" but that this name was given me in the night in the confusion that then existed and that the affiant for reasons then did not wish to make the correction.

A. O. Sorbel.

Subscribed and sworn to before me this 8th day of August 1929.

Andrew Hedman
Andrew Hedman,
Notary Public.

My commission
expires 8-10-30.

Affidavit Asle signed to prove who he was and what he did. *Courtesy of* From Norway to Home *and Harold's Photography, Sioux Falls, South Dakota.*

> *I can remember him walking off across the lawn and getting in Hank's Model T and driving off. That was the last time I saw him alive. About 10:30 am on Monday morning, John called out to the farm and told Mom that Grandpa had had a heart attack and died....It was my first encounter with death of anyone close in the family and it affected me quite deeply....The following days were sad days.*[18]

Asle Oscar Sorbel was seventy-one years, four months and two days old at the time of his death. He was buried in the Webster cemetery.

As South Dakota winds blow over lonely gravestones and memories fade, will Doc A.O. Sorbel and his historic role be remembered?

EPILOGUE

ASLE OSCAR SORBEL REMEMBERED

Do you remember the 21st night of September?
Love was changing the mind of pretenders.
—Earth, Wind & Fire

Alse's family and descendants knew little, if anything, about the role their father and grandfather played in the capture of the infamous Younger brothers' outlaw gang in 1876. What Asle had shared with his precious wife, Minnie, there is only speculation; whatever she knew, she kept to herself. The big secret was not hers to share.

After Asle's death, Minnie eventually moved into the Fiksdal apartments in Webster.

> *She had a one room apartment which she kept in immaculate condition. She would walk daily, several blocks to the post office to pick up her mail, even though there was some home delivery in Webster. She used that as an excuse to get outside each day for exercise. She regularly attended her church, read her Bible, and never missed the Paul Harvey newscast! As was true in her younger years, her hands were never idle, she knit mittens, crocheted afghans, and sewed rags for woven rugs. In the summer she kept a small garden beside the apartment building. This, she tended at five in the morning. She said to me once, "Early mornings are the most beautiful time of the day, just me, the birds and God."*

> *Tomina (Minnie) Westgaard Sorbel died on the 1st of April, 1954 after several days of hospitalization at the Webster Peabody Hospital. She apparently had been in pain with cancer for some time prior to her hospitalization, but the family was not aware of it. She was buried beside her husband and son Donald Kenneth, in the Webster Cemetery.*[1]

When Asle's death was made public, a testimonial by T.L. Vought (son of one of the Magnificent Madelia Seven) recalled,

> *Many times I have been at Webster and visited with this man, always something new to talk about. It was a pleasure supreme to visit at the hospitable home, not only to talk over by-gone days as those born and raised in the same community love to do, but to meet the good wife and the talented and good looking sons and daughters. The more I knew Mr. Sorbel, the more I dug deep under the so-called rough exterior and found him to be what he really was, a tender-hearted fellow. A true friend.*[2]

T.L. Vought's accolade is one of only a few accounts in which A.O.'s contemporaries remembered and praised the old and respected veterinarian. After A.O.'s revelation of the big secret in his 1924 letter to the *Argus Leader* and 1929 letter to editor C.L. Weicht of the *Northfield News*, the drama swirling around Asle's fearless ride would disappear—more or less—a dandelion seed in the wind.

But in recent years, a renewed resurgence of interest in the Jesse James/ Younger brothers' escapades has reawakened the public's fascination!

Antiquity miners researching the Northfield raid and the fiasco that followed have dug up shy, buried nuggets. One of those nuggets uncovered is this narrative. Lying quietly in a lode of gold, unearthed, it has caught the public's eye—and pen. The rest of the story is presently being appreciated, archived and celebrated. Family members, history aficionados, local Madelia and Webster citizens, Old West story enthusiasts, Northfield historians, Westerners Internationalists, Chautauqua speakers, humanities scholars and storytellers are presenting, telling, writing and smiling broadly.

Will Asle Oscar Sorbel be remembered? For short or long? Now hear this: Asle's story is presently being revived and cemented into local history by an annual Madelia, Watonwan County–wide drama. History aficionados are writing poetry. Family descendants have chronicled remembrances and scratched out memoirs and posted blogs. Collectively, historical events, married to the humanities and arts, are portraying an excited, eager farm boy, bent on an adventure—an adventure he never in his most fanciful predilections could have imagined. Finally, his life and times bring down the curtain on the final scene of the Jesse James/Younger brothers outlaw gang.

The resilience of history is stubborn. It refuses to disappear.

In 1948, the citizens of Northfield remembered. They began what would be known as the Defeat of Jesse James Days (DJJD). They would celebrate neither the romance nor glory of outlawry but honor the brave Northfield resisters while giving tribute to the memory of noble Joseph Heywood. Every year, September 4–8, reclusive Northfield, Minnesota, becomes a grand flamboyant city stage. Reenactors relive the events of the Northfield bank raid with unrestrained bravado and bluster.

Over nearly a week, 250,000 locals and tourists see a robbery bungled, six outlaws escaping on horseback amid smoking guns and the thunder of hooves. Dust swirling on the streets. Curses shouted. Horse sweat and acrid smells fouling the air. The Defeat of Jesse James Days in Northfield, Minnesota, has become a permanent fixture delighting, educating and enchanting all ages. The year 2022 marks the seventh-fourth festival.

Not to be eclipsed or dwarfed by DJJD in Northfield, Madelia citizens revived their history too, by telling "the rest of the story." Bearded gents, fashionable ladies, guns galore, mares and stallions properly saddled, harnessed and hitched and anyone intrigued by pageantry join in the fun. Reenactors bring to life the Capture of the Younger Brothers Gang Days (CYBGD) every year in late September.

Sauntering down main street Madelia, ladies parade in plumed hats and period dresses. Men walk about in Stetsons with guns holstered. Suddenly, horses gallop out of town and toward the shootout site south of La Salle (called Hanska Slough).

And in the middle of it all is that seventeen-year-old lad Asle—dressed in muddy, rumpled clothes, doing his valiant part, shouting, "The robbers are here, get your guns!"

The Younger Brothers Capture History Fest is held at Watona Park and Watonwan County Historical Center in Madelia. The following typical events tickle kids and amuse the adults: Historic Trolley Tours, Golf Round Up, Robbers on the Run/Walk, Vintage Baseball and Youth Baseball, Classic Car and Antique Show, Dave Ringen's Western Memorabilia, Open

Mural of the last stand of the Younger brothers gang painted on a west wall in downtown Madelia. *Courtesy of Anna Haase, Preferred Printing, Madelia, Minnesota.*

House Watonwan County Historical Center, Bank Robbery and Capture of the Younger Brothers Gang, Cow Pie Toss, Pony Rides, Petting Zoo, Horse Shoe Hunt, the Oscar Sorbel Hometown Hero Award, Steak Fry, Square Dancing and the Canyon Cowboys Band.

In 1998, Evertt Christensen of Madelia commemorated the capture of the Younger brothers by commissioning three brothers, Ryan, Craig and Jon Sweer, to paint a mural on the west wall of his brick building. Evertt's building at Main and Benzel Avenue SW, built in 1872, was thought to be the oldest brick structure in Watonwan County. The mural spans the entire side of the building. The mural was designed as a window into the past. It depicts the furious gun battle just before the capture of the Younger brothers. A historical marker near the mural stands as a sentinel, reading, "On September 21, 1876, Asle Oscar Sorbel, a seventeen year old Madelia farm boy alerted Sheriff James Glispin and Captain W.W. Murphy that the Northfield bank robbers were near."[3]

A local Madelia resident, the late Rex McBeth, an enthusiastic promoter of the annual Capture of the Younger Brothers Days celebration, wrote the following poem, which would have made Doc Sorbel smile:

Ode to Charlie Pitts

For fourteen days they fought their way, hungry, wet and cold
Til on September 21st Pitt's final tale was told
He stayed true to his friends to the very end
And they knew that's what he'd do
And it took five hits to kill Charlie Pitts,
down in Hanska slough.[4]

"On July 25, 2004, eleven of thirteen grandchildren of A.O. and Minnie Sorbel gathered with other descendants of his Norwegian immigrant parents to dedicate a new historic marker, a mile east of Hanska, Minnesota, just a short distance from where the family cabin had been where young Sorbel recognized the robbers."[5]

This historical marker is located on County Road 257, near the Northwest bank of Lake Linden. The inscriptions reads:

> *ASLE SORBEL'S RIDE*
> *IN 1854 OLE AND GURI SORBEL IMMIGRATED TO ROCK COUNTY WISCONSIN FROM HALLINGDAL, NORWAY. IN 1856 THEY SETTLED TO YOUR RIGHT ON THE NORTHWEST BANK OF LAKE LINDEN. ON SEPTEMBER 21, 1876, BOB, COLE AND JIM YOUNGER AND CHARLIE PITTS RECEIVED BREAKFAST FROM THE SORBELS. ASLE (OSCAR) SORBEL, AGE 17, WAS CONVINCED THE VISITORS WERE PART OF THE JAMES–YOUNGER GANG THAT ROBBED A NORTHFIELD MINNESOTA BANK. HE MOUNTED A WORKHORSE AND RODE 13 MILES TO MADELIA, MINNESOTA TO ALERT AUTHORITIES. A POSSE CAPTURED THE OUTLAWS NEAR LASALLE.*
> *ERECTED BY THE FAMILY OF OLE AND GURI SORBEL—2004.*[6]

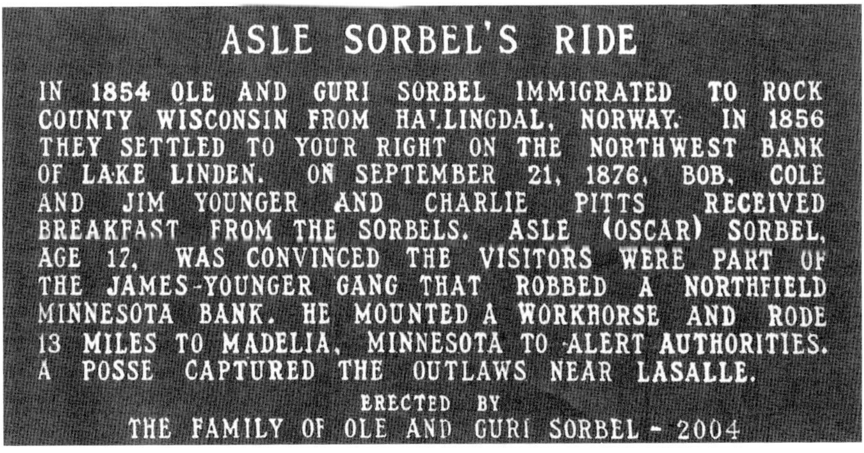

Historic marker text. *Courtesy of author.*

Asle Sorbel's marker placed by descendants in 2004. *Courtesy of K. Linzmeier, July 30, 2013.*

OSCAR SORBEL
Hometown Hero Award
Sponsored by Younger Brothers Capture Committee

MADELIA
MINNESOTA
"Pride of the Prairie"

Presented to

James Eiselt

In recognition of outstanding volunteer contributions to the community of Madelia, you have been selected as the 2014 Hometown Hero.

Mayor

Bob Yurcek, President of Younger Brothers Capture Committee

Presented September 2014

Typical Oscar Sorbel Hometown Hero Award. *Courtesy of Watonwan County Historical Society and Anna Haase, Preferred Printing, Madelia, Minnesota.*

This Sorbel historic marker joins earlier historic markers such as the monument with the inscription, "Site of Capture of the Younger Brothers, erected by the Watonwan County Historical Society in 1976." This was established on the 100th anniversary of the Northfield raid in 1876. This marker is located on Township Road 108, 0.3 miles from Minnesota state Highway 3.

The Watonwan County Museum proudly displays historical artifacts, books, photos, revolvers, long guns and memorabilia of the shootout, capture and roles Asle Sorbel and the Madelia citizenry played.

Each year since 1999, the Madelia Chamber of Commerce selects and then announces the Oscar Sorbel Hometown Hero Award as a part of the Younger Brothers Capture Event Festival. The intent of this award is to honor an individual who has served the Madelia community by his or her outstanding volunteering services. Winners to this point are Carol Etter, Joe McCabe, Millie Jacobson, Marv Davis, Rosemary Murphy, Jim Jose, Greg Cook, Katy Eiselt, Mike Grote, Bruce Nelson, Gloria Eager, Roy McCabe, Richard Block, Emilio Campo Jr., Shari Kilmer, Traci Henry,

"Sorbel" name fixed in blue tile of the former Reuben Sorbel Shoe Store on St. Joseph Street, downtown Rapid City, South Dakota. *Photo by Pam Fadness.*

James Eiselt, Colette Stone, Everett Christensen, Adeline Yates and Chuck Gunderson in 2019.[7]

This book, along with other publications (several listed in this bibliography), will hopefully and respectfully add to the resurgence of interest in this slice of western history and Americana. And most important of all, it recognizes and commemorates the courageous ride and life of a seventeen-year-old lad who did his best.

Try to remember the kind of September when life was slow
and oh, so mellow.

—The Fantastics

NOTES

Introduction

1. Tasker, *Early History of Lincoln County*, 220.
2. Koblas, *Jesse James Ate Here*.

Prologue: America Bound

1. From the minutes of a Linden Lutheran congregational meeting.

1. Mayhem Ninety Miles East

1. Gardner, *Shot All to Hell*, 73.
2. Ibid., 68.
3. Huntington, *Robber and Hero*, 15.
4. Ibid., 18.
5. Gardner, *Shot All to Hell*, 79.
6. Brant, *Outlaw Youngers*, 183.

2. *Tranquility at Ole's Farm—Drama in the Woods*

1. Fanebust, *Chasing Frank and Jesse James*, 51.
2. Ibid., 50.
3. Rølvaag, *Giants in the Earth*, 34.
4. Ibid., 37.
5. Croy, *Cole Younger*, 121, 122.
6. Brant, *Outlaw Youngers*, 188.
7. Fanebust, *Chasing Frank and Jesse James*, 52.
8. Younger, *Story of Cole Younger by Himself*, 82.
9. Koblas, *Jesse James Ate Here*, 177.
10. Brant, *Outlaw Youngers*, 192.
11. *Daily Press and Dakotian* (Yankton, SD), September 13, 1876.
12. *Mankato (MN) Free Press*, obituary, June 15, 1906.
13. *Mankato (MN) Record*, September 16, 1876.
14. Ted P. Yeatman, September 16, 1876. Noted in Fanebust, *Chasing Frank and Jesse James*, 66.
15. Huntington, *Robber and Hero*, 58.
16. Fanebust, *Chasing Frank and Jesse James*, 68.
17. Rølvaag, *Giants in the Earth*, 428, 429.

3. *Asle's "Paul Revere" Ride*

1. Gardner, *Shot All to Hell*, 148.
2. Ibid., 149
3. "Blunder of Hoy," *Faribault Republican*, September 20, 1876, 3.
4. Gardner, *Shot All to Hell*, 153.
5. Koblas, *Minnesota Grit*, 78.
6. Sorenson, "Story of Part."
7. Oscar Sorbel obituary, *Northfield News*, July 25, 1930.
8. Derome, "Story of How Younger Brothers Were Nabbed."
9. Ibid.
10. Ibid.
11. "Hanska Community Centennial Memorial," *Hanska Herald*, March 18, 1949, in the papers of Inga Sorbel; *Mankato Free Press*, May 20, 1993, as told by Nettie (Sorbel) Asleson.
12. Parsons, "Madelia's Paul Revere," 2.
13. Derome, "Story of How Younger Brothers Were Nabbed."

14. Ibid.
15. Fanebust, *Chasing Frank and Jesse James*, 73.

4. Asle's Role in the Shootout on the Watonwan

1. Koblas, *Minnesota Grit*, 29.
2. *Mankato (MN) Weekly Review*, September 26, 1876.
3. Yates, *Before Their Identity*, vii.
4. Ibid.
5. Koblas, *Jesse James Ate Here*, 219.
6. Yates, *Before Their Identity*, vii.
7. *Madelia (MN) Times Messenger*, August 27, 1904.
8. Sorenson, "Story of Part"; Steil, "Following the Trail."
9. Gardner, *Shot All to Hell*, 158.
10. Yates, *Before Their Identity*, 9.
11. Huntington, *Robber and Hero*, 67.
12. Yates, *Before Their Identity*, 9.
13. Gardner, *Shot All to Hell*, 161.
14. Ibid.
15. Younger, *Story of Cole Younger by Himself.*
16. *Gun Fighters*, 53.
17. Younger, *Story of Cole Younger by Himself.*
18. Steil, "Following the Trail."
19. Gardner, *Shot All to Hell*, 165
20. *Martin County Sentinel* (Faribault, MN), October 6, 1876.

5. A Chew of Tobacco and "Why That's the Boy"

1. Gardner, *Shot All to Hell*, 164–65.
2. Bronaugh, *The Youngers' Fight for Freedom*, 1906.
3. Armstong, "Recollections of a Nine-Year-Old Boy."
4. Huntington, *Robber and Hero*, 74.
5. *Review* (Mankato, MN), September 26, 1876.
6. *Northfield (MN) News*, Saturday, July 10, 1897.
7. *Review* (Mankato, MN), September 26, 1876.
8. Ibid.

9. Derome, "Story of How Younger Brothers Were Nabbed."
10. *Review* (Mankato, MN), September 26, 1876.
11. "Capture of the Youngers Recalled," *Rural News*, July 17, 1924.
12. Gardner, *Shot All to Hell*, 170; *Saint Paul Dispatch*, September 23, 1876; *Minneapolis Tribune*, September 23, 1877.
13. Gardner, *Shot All to Hell*, 172.
14. Vought, "As Boy and Man."
15. Koblas, *Minnesota Grit*, 78, 79; Sorenson, "Story of Part."
16. Koblas, *Minnesota Grit*, 79–80; *Mankato Free Press*, September 20, 1979.
17. Koblas, *Minnesota Grit*, 17–18; George A. Bradford letter to D.E. Hasey, January 20, 1924, copy in John Koblas collection.
18. Koblas, *Minnesota Grit*, 55; *Madelia (MN) Times-Messenger*, August 27, 1904.
19. Koblas, *Minnesota Grit*, 70.
20. Yates, *Seventy Five Years on the Watonwan*, 157.
21. Koblas, *Minnesota Grit*, 32.

6. Asle Visits His Nemesis in Stillwater Prison

1. Smith, *Last Hurrah of the James-Younger Gang*, 178.
2. Yates, *Before their Identity*, 21.
3. Brant, *Outlaw Youngers*, 212–13.
4. Croy, *Cole Younger*, 96.
5. Henry, *Jesse James*, 301–2.
6. Smith, *Last Hurrah of the James-Younger Gang*, 178.
7. Koblas, *When the Heavens Fell*, 21.
8. Ibid., 23.
9. Younger, *Story of Cole Younger by Himself*, 81.
10. Koblas, *When the Heavens Fell*, ix, 21.
11. Yates, *Seventy Five Years on the Watonwan*, 157.
12. Croy, *Cole Younger*, 160.
13. Koblas, *When the Heavens Fell*, 19.
14. *St. Paul & Minneapolis (MN) Pioneer Press-Tribune*, September 23, 1876.
15. J. Sorbel, "Sorbels Then and Now."
16. Harpstead, "Norway to Home," 16.
17. Yates, *Before Their Identity*, 25.
18. Brant, *Outlaw Youngers*, 246.
19. Ibid.
20. Ibid., 227.

21. "Youngers Are Out of Prison," *St. Paul Pioneer Press*, July 15, 1901.

7. Asle on the Run

1. *Madelia (MN) Times*, October 6, 1876.
2. D. Sorbel, interview, from Rapid City, ring conservator.
3. In a letter to the editor of the *Webster Journal*, July 31, 1930,
4. Vought, "Memories of Stirring Times."
5. D. Sorbel, "Recollections."
6. Huntington, *Robber and Hero*, 100.
7. Asle Oscar Sorbel letter to editor Carl Weicht of the *Northfield News*.
8. Ibid.
9. Ibid.
10. D. Sorbel, "Recollections."
11. Yates, *Before Their Identity*, 25.
12. Breihan, *Ride the Razor's Edge*, 239.

8. A Sudden Reappearance

1. Helmer, *History of Day County*.
2. Ochsenreiter, *History of Day County*.
3. Helmer, *History of Day County*.
4. Harpstead, "Norway to Home," 1980.
5. Ibid.
6. Ibid.
7. Ibid.
8. Ibid.
9. Ibid.
10. Ibid.
11. Cantrell, *Younger's Fatal Blunder*, 128–29.
12. Younger, *Story of Cole Younger by Himself*, 92.
13. Hedback, "Cole Younger's Story."
14. Heilbron and Younger, *Convict Life at the Minnesota State Prison*, 147.
15. Bronaugh, *Youngers' Fight for Freedom*, 319–20.
16. Harpstead, "Norway to Home," 33.
17. Ibid., 34.

18. "In the Matter of the Parole of Coleman and James Younger."
19. *Kansas City Star*, July 11,1901.
20. *Minneapolis (MN) Journal*, July 10, 1901.
21. *Butler Weekly Times*, July 18, 1901.

9. Dueling Banjos—Asle and Cole

1. Koblas, *Great Cole Younger*, 6.
2. Washington County Historical Society Files, Stillwater.
3. *Mankato Free Press*, March 18, 1902.
4. Harpstead, "Norway to Home," 34.
5. Ibid.
6. Olson, conversation.
7. D. Sorbel, "Recollections."
8. R. Sorbel letter to Oscar Lindholm, January 29, 1988.
9. Olson, conversation.
10. *Nashville American*, June 2, 1903.
11. Brant, *Jesse James*, 254; Settle, *Jesse James Was His Name*, 164; James, "Frank James," 9; Koblas, *Great Cole Younger*, 84.
12. *Minneapolis Journal*, February 23, 1902.
13. Reedstrom, "Cole Younger and Frank James Wild West Show," 31.
14. Koblas, *Great Cole Younger*, 90, 91.
15. *Knoxville Sentinel*, June 15, 1903.
16. Harpstead, "Norway to Home," 34.
17. Ibid.
18. Ibid.
19. Ibid., 38.
20. Gruby, interview. Babe was Oscar Lindholm's sister.

10. The Dance Continues

1. *Chillicothe Daily Democrat*, November 19, 1904.
2. Gardner, *Shot All to Hell*, 239–40.
3. Harpstead, "Norway to Home," 38.
4. Ibid.
5. Ibid., 35.
6. Yeatman, *Frank and Jesse James*, 319; Brant, *Jesse James*, 258–59.

7. Breihan, "Day Quantrill Burned Lawrence," 14.
8. Harpstead, "Norway to Home," 35.
9. Actual transcript copy of "What Life Has Taught Me," obtained from Bernice Lander, rancher from Edgemont, South Dakota, to the Arley Fadness Collection in 2016.
10. *Hot Springs Star*, July 7, 1911.
11. *Hot Springs Star*, December 29, 1911.
12. Younger, "What Life Has Taught Me."
13. Ibid.
14. Hovland, interview. August Hovland's grandson, Brad Hovland, of Rapid City, South Dakota, provided photos of Brad's father, August, and mother, Gena, from Ortley, South Dakota, who were horse clients of Doc. A.O. Sorbel.
15. Larson, interview. Paul Larson of Custer, South Dakota, provided a photo of Paul's father, Oscar Larson and grandfather Ivar Larson, who were Percheron horse clients of Doc A.O. Sorbel.
16. Younger, "What Life Has Taught Me."
17. Harpstead, "Norway to Home," 39.
18. Ibid.
19. Brant, *Jesse James*, 258–59.
20. Ibid.
21. George, *Conversion of Cole Younger*.
22. Gardner, *Shot All to Hell*.
23. Brant, *Outlaw Youngers*, 309–30.
24. Cantrell, *Youngers' Fatal Blunder*, 143.
25. Huntley, *Cole Younger*, 27.

11. Denouement: The Big Secret Revealed

1. Harpstead, "Norway to Home," 40.
2. Newspaper clipping, Northfield Public Library, newspaper unknown, dated March 22, 1916.
3. Koblas, *Great Cole Younger*, 223.
4. Ibid.
5. Harpstead, "Norway to Home," 39.
6. Ibid.
7. Ibid., 40.
8. Ibid., 41.

9. Ibid.
10. Data from St. John's Lutheran Church archives and Harpstead, "Norway to Home."
11. D. Sorbel, "Recollections."
12. Ibid.
13. Ibid.
14. Derome, "Story of How the Younger Brothers Were Nabbed."
15. Ibid.
16. Harpstead, "Norway to Home," attachment.
17. Copy from granddaughter Evelyn Sorbel Boyer.
18. D. Sorbel, "Recollections."

Epilogue

1. Harpstead, "Norway to Home," 12.
2. "Memories," *Webster Journal*, July 31, 1930.
3. The FreePress, Dan Greenwood, dgreenwood@mankatofreepress.com, August 22, 2019.
4. Steil, "Following the Trail."
5. Hvistendahl, "Sorbel Granddaughters Shed New Light."
6. Historical Marker Database, hmdb.org.
7. Schulz, interview. Madelia Chamber of Commerce, November 2019.

BIBLIOGRAPHY

Books

Bartos, Bob. *Memories of the Millennium*. Sioux Falls, SD: Pine Hill Press, 2000.

———. *New Memories of the Millennium Two.* Sioux Falls, SD: Pine Hill Press, 2002.

Blegen, Theodore C. *Norwegian Migration to America, 1825–1860.* Vol. 1. Northfield, MN: Norwegian-American Historical Association, 1931.

———. *Norwegian Migration to America, 1825–1860*. Vol. 2 Northfield, MN: Norwegian-American Historical Association, 1940.

Brant, Marley. *Jesse James: The Man and the Myth*. New York: Berkley Books, 1998.

———. *Outlaw Youngers: A Confederate Brotherhood*. Lanham, MD: Madison Books, 1992.

Breihan, Carl W. *Ride the Razor's Edge: The Younger Brothers Story*. Gretna, LA: Pelican Publishing Company, 1992.

Bronough, W.C. *The Youngers' Fight For Freedom*. Columbia, MO: E.W. Stephens Publishing, 1906.

Cantrell, Dallas. *Youngers' Fatal Blunder: Northfield, Minnesota*. Naylor Co., 1973.

Croy, Homer. *Cole Younger: The Last of the Great Outlaws*. New York: New American Library, 1958.

Fadness, Arley. *Balloons Aloft: Flying South Dakota Skies*. Maitland, FL: Xulon Press, 2013.

Fanebust, Wayne. *Chasing Frank and Jesse James: The Bungled Northfield Bank Raid Robbery and Long Manhunt.*

Floren, Myron, and Randee Floren. Accordion Man. Brattleboro, VT: Stephan Green Publisher, 1981.

Gardner, Mark Lee. *Shot All to Hell: Jesse James, the Northfield Raid, and the Wild West's Greatest Escape*. New York: William Morrow, 2013.

George, Todd M. *The Conversion of Cole Younger: The Early Day Bandit*. January 1, 1963.

The Gun Fighters. Alexandria, VA: Time-Life Books, 1974.

Hageneder, Fred. *The Meaning of Trees, Botany, History, Healing, Lore*. San Francisco: Chronicle Books, 2006.

Heilbron, W.C., and Cole Younger. *Convict Life at the Minnesota State Prison*. St. Paul, MN: W.C. Heilbron, 1909.

Helmer, Lavonne Jones. *History of Day County*. Aberdeen, SD: North Plain Press, 1981.

Henry, Will. *Jesse James: Death of a Legend*. New York: Leisure Books, 1996.

Huntington, George. *Robber and Hero: The Story of the Northfield Bank Raid*. St. Paul: Minnesota Historical Society Press, 1986.

Huntley, A. *Cole Younger, Famous Outlaws of the West*. Fall 1964, p. 27. Jefferson, NC: McFarland & Company Inc., 2017.

Koblas, John J. *The Great Cole Younger and Frank James Historical Wild West Show*. St. Cloud, MN: North Star Press Inc., 2002.

———. *Jesse James Ate Here, An Outlaw Tour and History of Minnesota at the Time of the Northfield Raid*. St. Cloud, MN: North Star Press Inc., 2001.

———. *Minnesota Grit: The Men Who Defeated the James-Younger Gang*. St. Cloud, MN: North Star Press Inc., 2005.

———. *When The Heavens Fell: The Youngers in Stillwater Prison*. St. Cloud, MN: North Star Press Inc., 2002.

Krause, Herbert. *Wind Without Rain*. Indianapolis, IN: Bobbs-Merrill Company, 1939.

Longfellow, Henry Wadsworth. *Tales of a Wayside Inn*. Boston: Ticknor and Fields, 1863.

McLachlan, Sean. *The Last Ride of the James-Younger Gang: Jesse James and the Northfield Raid, 1876*. London: Osprey Publishers, 2012.

Ochsenreiter, L.G. *History of Day County (1873–1926)*. Mitchell, SD: Educator Supply Company, 1926.

Potter, Theodore Edgar. *Capture of the Younger Brothers*. Berrien Springs, MI: Hardscrabble Books, 1913.

Oyos, Lynwood E. *We Would See Jesus: Augustana Academy 1869–1971*. Sioux Falls, SC: Pine Hill Press, 2006.

Quist, B. Wayne. *The History of the Christdala Evangelical Church.* Dundas, MN: Small World Press, 1994.

Reedstrom, E. Lisle. "The Cole Younger and Frank James Wild West Show." *True West* 39, no. 10 (October 1992).

Rølvaag, Ole E. *Giants in the Earth*. New York: Harper and Row, 1963.

Rynnings, Ole. *True Account of America*. Classic Reprint Series, 2017.

Settle, William, Jr. *Jesse James Was His Name*. Lincoln: University of Nebraska Press, 1966.

Smith, Robert Barr. *The Last Hurrah of the James-Younger Gang*. Norman: University of Oklahoma Press, 2001.

Tasker, A.E. *Early History of Lincoln County, From the Early Writings of Old Pioneers, Historians, and Later Writers* Lake Benton, MN: Lake Benton News Print, 1936.

Wilson, J.E. *The Wild Bandits of the Border, A Thrilling Story of the Adventures and Exploits of Frank and Jesse James.* Chicago: Laird & Lee Publishers, 1893.

Yates, Buster. *Seventy Five Years on the Watonwan*. Madelia, MN, 1986.

Yates, Ruth Rentz. *Before Their Identity*. Madelia, MN, 1996.

Yeatman, Ted P. *Frank and Jesse James: The Story Behind the Legend.* Nashville, TN: Cumberland House, 2000.

Younger, Cole, *The Story of Cole Younger by Himself, Being an Autobiography of the Missouri Guerrilla Captain and Wild West Outlaw, Partner of Jesse James, and His Capture and Prison Life.* St. Paul, Minnesota Historical Society Press, 2000.

Newspapers, Articles, Notes and Letters

Breihan, Carl W. "The Day Quantrill Burned Lawrence." *The West*, January 1972.

Derome, J.A. "A Story of How the Younger Brothers Were Nabbed." (Sioux Falls, SD). March 22–June 4, 1924.

Hvistendahl, Susan. "Sorbel Granddaughters Shed New Light on Post-Raid Hero." *Scriver Scribbler*, Spring 2006.

James, Thurston. "Frank James—The Post-Outlaw Years." *James-Younger Gang Journal* (Spring 2001): 9.

New Ulm Journal. "History of Nora Universal Unitarian Church." August 20, 2000.

Parsons, Chuck. "Madelia's Paul Revere—Nemesis of the Younger Gang." *The English Westerners Tally Sheet* 23, no. 30 (April 1977): 2.

Sorbel, Reuben. Letter to Oscar Lindholm, January 29, 1988. Compliments to Lindholm's daughter, Myrna Wey of Green Mountain, Colorado.

Sorbel Tape Transcription. Participants: Susan Hvistendahl, Mary Sorbel Harpstead, Dale Harpstead, Evelyn Sorbel Boyer, Earl Weinmann, Chip DeMann, John Klobas, Maggie Lee and Thomas Boyer, Northfield Historical Society, April 2, 2006.

Sorenson, Franklin L. "Story of Part Which Norwegian Lad Took in Capturing the Notorious Younger Bros." Undated *Blue Earth Post* article, Watonwan Historical Society, Madelia.

Steil, Mark. "Following the Trail of Jesse James." Minnesota Public Radio. September 7, 2001. http://news.minnesota.publicradio.org/features/200109/07_steilm_jamesgang-m/.

Vought, T.L. "As Boy and Man." *Webster (SD) Journal*. July 17, 1930.

———. "Memories of Stirring Times—Sorbel Stopped the Men of Crimes." *Webster (SD) Journal*, July 31, 1930.

Younger, Cole. "What Life Has Taught Me." Notes from a speech delivered at the Grand Theater in Hot Springs, South Dakota, July 10, 1911. Copy of speech compliments to this author by Edgemont, South Dakota rancher Bernice Landers in 2017.

Unpublished Manuscripts, Blogs and Websites

Armstrong, Charles. "Recollections of a Nine-Year-Old Boy Concerning Events Following the Northfield Bank Robbery." Northfield, Minnesota, Bank Robbery of 1876. Selected Manuscripts Collections and Government Records. Microfilm Edition. Minnesota Historical Society.

Harpstead, Mary. "Norway to Home." Unpublished journal (memoir), 1980. Used by permission.

Hedback, A.E., M.D. "Cole Younger's Story of the Northfield Raid in his Own Handwriting." June 7, 1921.

"In the Matter of the Parole of Coleman and James Younger." Northfield, Minnesota, Bank Robbery of 1876. Selected Manuscripts Collections and Government Records, Microfilm Edition, Roll 4, Minnesota Historical Society.

Linden Lutheran Church booklet by J.S. Helling as told to Sorbel in "The Sorbels Then and Now," 1982. Used by permission.

Midwest Weekends. "Posse on the Prairie." December 28, 2017. https://midwestweekends.com/plan-a-trip/history-heritage/frontier-history/madelia-jesse-james/.

Nelson, Leonard. Five Generations Chart. St. James, Minnesota, February 1982.

Sorbel, David Martin. "Recollections: At 65 Years Plus." Unpublished manuscript, 1984.

Sorbel, Jan. "The Sorbels Then and Now." Unpublished memoir, 1982.

William Watts Folwell and Family Papers, Northfield, (Minnesota) Bank Robbery of 1876: Selected Manuscripts Collections and Government Records. Microfilm Edition. Minnesota Historical Society.

Interviews, Correspondences and Conversations

Boyer, Evelyn Sorbel. Conversation with the author.

Gruby, Bab. Interview with Oscar Akerson, who was a kid during the time of the Madelia shoot-out.

Hovland, Brad. Interview with the author, 2017.

Larson, Paul. Interview with the author, 2018.

Nielsen, Dorothy Sorbel. Conversation with the author.

Olson, Edith. Conversation with the author.

Rentschler, Oriette. Conversations with the author.

Schulz, Karla. Interview with the author.

Sorbel, Dan. Interviews with the author.

Sorbel, Herbert. Conversation with the author.

Sorbel, Robert. Conversations with the author.

Swartz, Robert. Correspondence with the author.

Woodring, Sally Gravenhurt. Telephone conversation with the author.

Private Collections

Dan Sorbel repository retains ownership of the "prize ring" Asle purchased with the reward money he (Asle) received for the capture of the Younger Brothers.

Sorbel family collections. Numerous photos and written materials.

Stanley Harpstead collection. Sorbel Bible and assorted photographs.

ABOUT THE AUTHOR

Arley Kenneth Fadness was born in Webster, Day County, South Dakota, the same hometown of Asle Oscar Sorbel. He married his wife, Pamela, in Madelia, Minnesota, where the Younger brothers were captured. The couple have four adult children—Tim, Susan, Joel and Rebekah—and one grandchild, Ela Rae.

Arley is a retired draftsman and clergy and active history enthusiast and writer. He drafted blueprints for the Bomarc Guided Missile, the 707 and KC135 aircrafts for Boeings in Seattle. He also drafted blueprints for architectural and engineering firms while a student at Augustana College and Luther Seminary. When Ed Yost, the inventor of the modern hot air balloon, needed a drafter for FAA balloon certifications, Arley joined the project and drew up blueprints for Ed's one-thousand- and five-hundred-cubic-meter gas balloon systems.

He attended McCormick Theological Seminary in Chicago, attaining a doctor of ministry degree focusing on parish revitalization. Dr. Fadness served parishes in Arizona, Minnesota, Wyoming and South Dakota. Arley is the author of several Lenten program books, published through CSS Publishing of Lima, Ohio, and a history of ballooning titled Balloons *Aloft: Flying South Dakota Skies*.

In 2020, his book *A Long, Long Road Back to Love*, which highlights the Parable of the Prodigal Son, was published by CSS Publishing.

As a hobby, Arley has restored a 1956 Thunderbird and a 1930 Model A Roadster.

Presently, Arley is a PowerPoint presenter of five history programs through the South Dakota Humanities as a Humanities Scholar.